MEN, HORSES, MUD AND STEW

MEN, HORSES, MUD AND STEW

THE LITTLE FUSILIER'S GREAT WAR

WILFRED COOK

EDITED BY AUDREY LARKINS

TOMMIES GUIDES

Tommies Guides
Menin House
13 Hunloke Avenue
Eastbourne
East Sussex
BN22 8UL

www.tommiesguides.co.uk
First published in Great Britain by Tommies Guides, 2009

ISBN 978-0 95556 984 5

Cover design by Tommies Guides
Typeset by Graham Hales, Derby
Printed and bound in Great Britain by CPI Antony Rowe,
Chippenham and Eastbourne

CONTENTS

INTRODUCTION

This is the story of Wilfred Cook (my Father) who volunteered for the army at the age of eighteen and left his home in Leeds in March 1915. After initial training in Whitley Bay he was transferred to the Northumberland Fusiliers (known as the Fighting Fifth). He tells how they were equipped and sent to France to reinforce the regiments already fighting there. They arrived first at Poperinghe from where they marched by night to join the battalion entrenched at St Eloi on the Ypres Salient.

He describes the conditions of 'Men, horses, mud and stew'. After a brief rest at Ouerdam they were sent to the notorious Sanctuary Wood where he was wounded for the first time. He then spent time guarding Bridge 14 on the Ypres Canal. He returned to St Eloi where he developed septic poisoning from a blister on his foot caused by the long marches. This time he was sent to a Military Hospital in Rouen where he spent his 19th birthday. The nursing sister called him her 'Little Fusilier', and he describes the excellent care he received there before returning to the trenches on the Ypres Salient. In another battle at St Eloi he captured 35 German prisoners.

Rather reluctantly he then became a bandsman and stretcher-bearer. There are many amusing accounts of his fellow bandsmen as well as the harrowing stories of his work as a stretcher-bearer.

On July 10th 1916 the battalion arrived on the Somme and was immediately in the thick of battle at 'Happy Valley', Delville Wood and Bazentin-le Petit where there were many casualties.

In April 1917 the battalion was involved in the battle of Arras where he was wounded again and was sent back to England where the treatment was not so good.

In March 1918 he returned to France and was transferred to the Field Survey Corps of the Royal Engineers. As a Sapper he was involved in setting up and manning Operation Posts in various locations from the top of a church steeple, an empty house, a deserted factory, a dugout or a captured pill-box. These posts were manned by two men day and night who pin-pointed the location of enemy guns and movement of troops reporting back to HQ at Boves near Amiens. The Germans were driven back over the Hindenburg Line but not before there were many battles and rearguard actions. Finally the news reached them that the Armistice was signed but it was February 1919 before he was finally demobbed.

This is an account of an ordinary fusilier who saw great suffering but kept his sense of humour and made some wonderful pals, many of whom died in the mud of Flanders fields.

Audrey Larkins

ABOUT THE ILLUSTRATIONS

The illustrations for this book were created by Soren Hawkes, a British Artist currently living in Ieper (know in this book as Ypres), Belgium. His Great Grandfather, Maurice Augustus Staunton served in the Lancashire Fusiliers during WW1 and his Great Uncle, Patrick Thomas Staunton served in 1st Battalion, the Welsh Regiment and was killed in action at a place called the 'Bluff' on the 20th February 1915 and is commemorated on the Menin Gate. The artist's studio overlooks the panel in which his name is listed.

From Saturday mornings at the age of 12, Soren began drawing at Camberwell College of Arts and from there went on to study at the City & Guilds of London Art School attaining a Foundation Diploma in Art and Design (with distinction).

Further education at the Camberwell College of Arts includes both BA (Hons) and Master of Arts.

He has exhibited at places such as The Royal Academy of Art (London), National Print Fair (Barbican), National Print Show (National Theatre) and Royal Academy of Arts.

Most recently he contributed to part of the BBC's 90th Anniversary commemorations of the end of the First World War in the genealogy programme 'My Family At War' with the actress Natalie Cassidy. Many of the illustrations inspired by and featuring in this book can now be obtained as prints by visiting the artist at his studio in Belgium or by visiting the website: www.passchendaeleprints.com

In addition to an excellent range of military books, maps and guides, the prints can also be ordered direct from Tommies Guides, Bookseller & Publisher at www.tommiesguides.co.uk

FOREWORD

The writer of this narrative has no 'acknowledgements' to make other than the help he gained by reading the 'History of the 1st and 2nd Battalions The Northumberland Fusiliers 1914-1918' by Brigadier H.R.E. Sandilands CMG, DSO, in checking names, dates and places visited and fought over by the 1st Battalion in France from August 14th 1914 to the end of hostilities.

The Brigadier's history is excellently compiled. This is a narrative from a man much less competent who served with the Battalion in those years and whose memory served him well in spite of the lapse of time. Everything in the following pages is true, only occasionally does it give anything second hand and then only after careful thought as to its possibility and truth.

After the war the writer paid several visits to many of the places named, the last being in 1983, when the ground had seen another holocaust. He visited the many cemeteries around Ypres where so many of his old comrades lie. Some of those recorded in the list of names of those with 'no known grave', he had seen die and in some cases actually attended their burial whilst the chaplain read the prayers and committed them to the elements and rest.

Nor does he feel that any apology is needed for the use of proper names, only using a nom-de-plume where the individual did not come up to the high standard of others mentioned, All societies have their like unfortunately. They are no disgrace to the regiment, only to themselves.

This account was written some years ago at the request of his son, (a captain in the Jat Regiment, Indian army, now deceased, who served through the Burma campaign). It is written to serve as a memorial to men of a regiment who are now incorporated in the Royal Regiment of Fusiliers by reorganisation of the new army. The men of the Northumberland Fusiliers earned their other title the 'Fighting Fifth' and this is to record some of their lives, their courage and discomfort, the latter being overcome by their own inimitable humour and spirit.

Wilfred Cook

If this book requires any dedication let it be to:

C.S.M. Drayson, Syd, Jackie, Hughie and men of 'X' company the First Battalion of the Northumberland Fusiliers, from 1914 to the end of the war.

CHAPTER ONE

LEAVING HOME

The declaration of war in August 1914 was no surprise to the boys in our family as we had been reading for some years past of the menace of the German nation, with its aspirations of overcoming the world, with England as its first objective. The arms race was on, with us having a navy second to none in numbers of ships and the quality of command protecting our Empire 'on which the sun never sets'.

Father encouraged us all to read, he being a prolific reader himself, principally works with a theological flavour. He was a Bible scholar of no mean standard, also a lover of Shakespeare, Tennyson, Byron, Gibbon and Spurgeon's Sermons for good measure. Ours was a truly Christian home, family prayers and chapel attendance the norm (Methodist). Mother in a quieter way endorsed his doctrine; her Bible still in my bookcase is marked and noted in her own hand. She never deviated from a Christian standard in which she reared a family of four boys and three girls.

We read, almost in secret, the current boy's magazines and papers, The Gem, Magnet, Marvel and Union Jack from their very first numbers at a halfpenny a copy for the first few weeks and then to a full one penny, never any more. For lighter moments after reading of Harry Wharton, Tom Merry, Billy Bunter and Sexton Blake, we read the comics; Chips, Lot-o-Fun, Funny Cuts etc. The local library added the works of Ballantyne, Stevenson, Marryatt and other excellent writers of voyages of discovery, adventure and history, all good stuff.

Only one was fully approved by Father, 'The Boy's Friend' edited by one Hamilton, which was an alias of the famous Frank Richards. His writing had a good moral background and readers were encouraged in healthy sport and good behaviour. There we learned through its serials the portents of the coming war.

'Britain Invaded', 'Britain at Bay' and finally 'Britain's Revenge' told the story of a German invasion with lurid line drawings of hordes of spiked helmeted enemies led by a Kaiser riding a charger, sword in hand. His waxed moustache accentuated his menacing appearance in Trafalgar Square with the figure of Nelson beneath his jackboots and a triumphant glow on his face. Of course, inevitably, in the final episode all is changed and the picture is of Germans on their knees begging for mercy and the Kaiser deposed. In a way it was a good forecast of what was to come – would that our politicians had heeded it then and later.

This was in our schooldays, but now by 1914 three of us had left school and had embarked on our future careers in a competitive world, where hours were long and wages low. We were ready to drop any vocation temporarily for the greater adventure when it came (of which we had little doubt).

Arthur the second son had already left his job as butcher's boy to join the navy. This had always been his ambition. He joined at the age of fifteen; nothing his parents said could deter him. After his year of training at 'Ganges' he was now in South American waters with HMS Hermoine. His career subsequently was a story of his rise from the lower decks to commissioned rank and a brilliant career in which we all took pride.

Jack my eldest brother was a grocer, well on his way to management. He would have preferred an outdoor life, being a very good footballer in his schooldays. He was tall, well built and the wit of the family, sometimes to the despair of his serious minded father, who once a grocer, had put him to the trade.

I was apprenticed as a printer and already considered myself worth much more than the paltry few shillings a week paid for fifty hours work.

When the call-up came, many young men enlisted with the sole idea of getting away from the factories and the monotony of labour for a mere pittance. The unemployed with no state aid saw the army as a means of being fed and clothed, yet in spite of all there was a strong patriotic feeling that this was the right thing to do and that our cause was just.

The summer of 1914 was a very good one with weeks of unbroken sunshine, but other clouds were gathering and they looked like war clouds. What news we got was from the daily papers with a 'Special Edition'. News boys running the streets around town cried "Special-assassination in Europe", "Mobilisation Ordered by Parliament", "Reserves Reporting" and finally on the 4th of August:

"Special! War Declared. Read all about it!"

Their papers were sold before the ink was dry, from city centres to the meanest streets and the excitement percolated everywhere.

It was a Bank Holiday week so those who could afford it were away on holiday. So far we had never enjoyed this luxury, along with thousands more. Our youngest brother Walter was camping at Scarborough with the Boy's Brigade. He returned home at once as he thought what money he had his Mother might need now war had started. How true he was to be.

Jack soon answered the call. By the end of August he was in the army. Father reassured Mother that there was no need to worry, the war would be over by Christmas. In spite of a naval victory in the North Sea we knew things were grim, our armies were totally outnumbered by men and equipment. It appeared that 'the thin red line' already fighting with their backs to the wall had little if anything different than they had in the recent Boer War which ended in 1902.

Earl Grey, the Home Secretary said, "The lights in Europe are going out." They were indeed, but still there were those who could not or would not see it, some already counting on the profits to be gained in supplying munitions and from the rapidly rising prices of all commodities at home. The services were purely voluntary, conscription a long way off as yet.

As the casualty lists began to appear in the papers, so did the recruiting posters on the hoardings, the most famous being Kitchener's pointing finger with the caption "Your Country Needs You." The recruiting Sergeants became more evident in City Square with their counterpart for the Navy offering 'the King's shilling' to likely men.

The Territorial Army, once looked upon as weekend soldiers, was called to the colours soon to be overseas. In spite of their original contract being that Foreign Service was to be voluntary, one never heard of a man invoking the clause. They were to be a vital force to join the regular soldiers, bearing the brunt of those early days fighting as men never fought before.

My fears were that the war would be over before I reached the age of enlistment, so like many more I joined under age, adding a year to my age to become nineteen. This was in March 1915 when I had been told that the recruiting officers had ceased asking for birth certificates and one's word was sufficient providing the physical condition supported it.

Saturday March 13th 1915 saw me in a queue at the local recruiting office facing a recruiting officer who seemed to me very efficient in disposing of naked men. With an order to bend down and touch my toes without bending my knees he gathered I would make a gymnast, meanwhile with a flashlight torch he inspected my rear anatomy. The stethoscope was applied to my chest with the command to say 'ninety nine' (why, I never did learn).

"A1...next man" and I retreated to dress again. The swearing in was duly performed as I held a Bible and said:

"I swear to defend my King and Country against all enemies, so help me God..." and was given a shilling to fasten the deal. On being asked what regiment I would like to join I had no hesitation in saying the West Yorks, it being my strong desire to serve in the infantry. In spite of all that came later I never regretted this and had my time to come again it would be the same.

With farewells said to those at home, my employer, friends and 'the girl I left behind me' I boarded the train to York. A number of passengers looked as if they were on the same errand, being the quota for the day from Leeds-quite a respectable one too considering that this is only to York. Others would be bound for Harwich, Portsmouth, Aldershot or wherever depots were. Most were dressed in working clothes, cloth caps with here and there a bowler or trilby. One had brought his umbrella; probably he hoped to become an officer. Even to my inexperienced eye, many looked anything but soldiers.

The reception at York station was by a sergeant of the West Yorks with Military Police assisting in checking warrants, seeing us formed up and marched off to Fulford Barracks. The residents of this old military city paid little attention to this motley crowd, no doubt a common sight, now that war was crying out for more and more men.

This narrative is mostly about men, individual men whom I have no desire ever to forget. I was treading the streets of York beside an old regular soldier of the W. Yorks returning to the colours. His reserve days were finished and he had volunteered to serve again. 'Spud' Murphy, for that was his name, given to me with the information that all Murphies were 'spuds' in the army and later I gathered that all 'spuds' were Murphies that we peeled sometimes for punishment and ate as potato mash. He was not the only man returning to the colours. They were easily recognised as they showed us how to form up before we set off in ranks of four and gave us little tips once we had entered the famous Barrack Gates at Fulford. The old soldiers must have been a great help to the staff in knocking us 'civvies' into shape. A report at the time said "Four out of five recruits had such bad teeth they could not eat properly, scarcely a third of all adult men could be said to have full normal health or strength."

In a barrack room we stood waiting for further instructions. The Corporal entered, a big red-faced individual full of his own importance. He stood in front of us and addressed the assembly but not before my friend Murphy whispered to me:

"This bloke is Tarper. He was a recruit when I left the Regiment"

"Now lads you are in the army now" Tarper said "This is your barrack room where you are under me for discipline and without me you'd get nothing worth having. I also see to wants such as blankets and kit and see you get fed proper, see!" We saw!

He continued "Now it is usual when recruits join the Regiment that they make a presentation to the corporal in charge of the barrack room in return for his favours. This is done by the passing round of an 'at, in which you drop your contribution."

There was a pause and silence.

"Well, go on," he says "Take off your 'at and pass it round." This to an individual who was standing with his trilby on his head looking quite awe-struck after this opening oration.

"Scrub it kid" Murphy whispered to me "He's not entitled, I'll get him for this" He ignored the hat when it reached us. I made a movement with an empty hand which sufficed but others contributed probably returning the King's shilling to one of his servants. Tarper meanwhile ran his eye over the fifty or more men in the room with a few quizzical glances at my new friend but no recognition of each other brought any comment.

The evening was spent pleasantly enough. Whilst there were many who chose to go to the local pubs or the canteen, there were sufficient of us to make a happy company in the barrack room, especially as we had music rendered by a 'Geordie' who had the foresight to bring his concertina. He was an expert, giving us a performance worthy of any audience and his humour with it equally so. It was a pity I lost track of that little fellow, he would find his niche and be welcomed.

Supper was to be had for those who cared to go to the cookhouse where a hot soup could be had free-evidently made from the leavings from the days main meal, with parts of the joint mainly gristle and bone, but not too bad. We welcomed it.

There was a little trouble later as the revellers returned but no one was seriously hurt. Apparently the beer in York had boxing gloves in it and loosened tongues a little too much.

Our conscientious corporal returned to see us all tucked in. He called the roll, his slur revealing that the contributions had been spent in the Corporal's mess bar. Spud Murphy had also been to the canteen and was just in the mood for tackling Tarper. He made no bones about it as he said: "Corporal Tarper, I remember you in India as a recruit and later as a rotten soldier, same as you are a rotten corporal now. You had these lads pass round an 'at against King's regulations. Tomorrow Tarper I'm reporting you an you'll lose them bleedin' stripes for it...I'll have you up at Orderly Room on a charge of corruption and taking bribes, with an old soldier bringing the charge or my name's not Murphy...yes, Murphy, Private number 64289 C.Company, 1st Battalion, India. You'll remember him."

Tarper's face was a study. He did some blustering but knew he had met his Waterloo as a Corporal and sure enough he lost his stripes next day and we had the satisfaction of seeing him at squad drill later. The West Yorkshire Regiment had a code of honour apparently for its NCOs.

The following day we were handed a full kit, everything a man could need apart from luxury, even down to a 'housewife', this being a convenient little pack of needles, wool, shirt and trouser buttons etc. but no instructions how to sew or darn. This we would learn by necessity, the mother of invention. Spared the indignity of a blue tunic, trousers and forage cap as earlier recruits had, we had khaki, with the exception of a greatcoat – a heavy blue vicuna cut in military style.

Immediately returning to our barrack room, the fitting completed, our greatest difficulty being the fitting of puttees which seemed to be yards too long, tempting one to cut them down a few feet. With Spud's help I finally learned the knack and with calves encased neatly down to my army boots I felt something like a deep-sea diver must with lead soles. Just to try them out, we paraded the huge barrack square, where we learned we have a right and a left hand, this being news to some who had difficulty, causing some confusion when a man took the wrong turning. It was weeks before we would be absolutely perfect as squads in this regard.

We learned too that every soldier, no matter his age or lack of puberty, had to shave daily without fail and to leave his top lip unshaved although I saw a lack of moustaches even on the instructors. The razor was an issue, being the shape of the old 'cut-throat' but the blade a piece of sharpened tin, yet it sufficed, with much scraping and sundry cuts. Had anyone used a safety razor he would have been labelled a 'sissy' but they never reached us as far as I can recall. They were a new American invention by a man named Gillette, whose portrait some of us had seen in adverts but treated with disdain.

Having been knocked into some sort of order, we were considered good enough to be seen in York itself, where uniformed men march with precision. By careful folding we packed everything into a huge kit bag and marched off to York station to entrain for Whitley Bay.

CHAPTER TWO
WHITLEY BAY

Arriving at our destination we had a good reception. Our York friends had not wasted time on us. We quickly formed ranks on the platform to be marched off to billets in the town or on the sea front. I was sent to a former café near the Spanish City Amusement park. Now we had neither Corporal Tarper nor his beds. The floorboards became our mattresses, our kit bags a pillow and two blankets to shelter us from a draught from the sea, which crept under the door. A few days of this and we had the added luxury of a palliasse filled with straw but no bedstead. Who cared? Sleep soon came to healthy bodies after the bracing North Sea air and plenty of exercise.

We had to sort ourselves out, select our immediate friends, like to like, and this was soon accomplished. My first real pal was a young man from Goole, a former ship's steward named Pratt – sturdy, cheerful and a great pal. He would be useful in trouble, which looked likely as there were one or two aggressive blokes ready to throw their weight about at the drop of a hat. The grouser was present of course. His grub was always lousy according to him, although he had to be held back at meal times from confiscating the lion's share. Pratt was good at such times and he flattened more than one as he collected our share. These individuals were sorted out and a few found themselves with a free pass to return to Civvy Street, not being considered fit for the service. Probably they would appear again with the stigma of conscript – we were volunteers and proud of it.

The language of a barrack room struck me like a thunderclap. Coming from a Christian home this was new to me and had no meaning but sheer vulgarity for the sake of it. Much of it was senseless and revealed the lack of vocabulary of the user. To protest was useless and sad to say many good sons picked up words and habits not taught at home. Here I must say this was the army, rough and tough, but it seeped into the language of the streets in later years and is not even barred from entertainment halls, radio and TV, much to our shame. My disgust made me determined not to succumb and I never did, earning for myself a nickname later, but showed me some respect from my friends. It saved me from many a quarrel, for although swearing was universal there were many occasions when 'you called me a ...' would provoke a fight. This broke many friendships, things might be patched up but some lasted and to lose a friend was a great loss. No one enjoyed being a loner much less in later days when pressures became much harder. I was always fortunate in having some good friend I could converse sensibly with. Pratt was the first and his death later was a grief I have never overcome. He was too good a lad to be lost to his decade, but then I premeditate the story.

'Square Bashing' or foot drill to be precise was on the promenade, the sands or the golf links all facing the sea. Nothing could be better for us, we thrived on it. Food was good even though we had no dining hall, as yet and we grew daily in strength and revelled in it.

Our instructors at Whitley Bay were excellent. If their intention was to make us efficient soldiers in a few weeks, then they certainly went the right way about it. Later experience and the years have convinced me that they worked on the right lines, no doubt the credit must go to their Commanding Officer Colonel Friend. To me he looked an old man but he had our full respect. He rode a horse magnificently and to see him taking a full parade was a proud sight.

Sergeant Pearson, a regular soldier and a gentleman led my platoon. He did not drive us but led by his example. In appearance he was always smartly dressed and scrupulously clean (his buttons alone were the envy of all.) To my knowledge he never used a coarse or wrong word, rather the reverse. On our first morning under him, speaking to us firmly but kindly, he won us all. I owe it to him that I became a first-class shot on the rifle range, for his musketry instructions were a model in themselves. He was Bisley standard. When we fired our proficiency test on the range after a few weeks he was lying beside me as I fired at the distant targets. Then came the supreme test, 15 rounds rapid fire at 400yds in one minute. My rifle was empty and lay beside me before the minute was up.

"I hope you've hit the target lad." he remarked "You've certainly made the time." They were there, fourteen bulls and one inner and at 'snapping targets' where the figure was exposed for only three seconds I succeeded in putting two bullets through one target and never had one miss.

"Who is that man on number four target?"

"Cook Sir" Pearson replied.

"Good man, best shooting of the day."

My heart swelled and I never felt so proud in my life. This skill I never lost and says much for Sgt. Pearson's instruction which I later used in training others.

The Company Sergeant Major, Bill Hodgson was also a man apart. Much is said of Sergeant Majors to their discredit but not of Bill, as we referred to him between ourselves. Tall and sturdy and taking probably size eleven in boots, he was a model of a man. Beneath that fierce exterior dwelt a warm heart and knowledge of men, particularly youngsters as many of us were. We moved under his command like automatons-nothing slipshod missed his eagle eye. His 'left-right-left' were emphasised by those size eleven's which punctuated the thunder of his voice. Nothing satisfied him until we all moved of one accord then "Halt-Order Arms-Stand Easy." Then he showed his humanity, lowering his voice he would come close to talk to us.

"Now lads that was pretty good. I know you think I shout a lot at you but it's all for your own good. You cannot work on poor words of command. Don't take it to heart, I mean no harm." looking at some poor individual almost in tears having been brought up behind a plough and to whom this is sheer agony.

"You will all make good soldiers and all this will become easy to you. Fall out for a few minutes."

He drew apart and had a few words with Sgt. Pearson. Whilst tab ends were produced for a quick draw and he moved to another platoon for their session. How right Bill was. A soldier works to words of command, without orders he is at sea. Seldom is he left to his own initiative, should he be he reflects what he has been taught and acts accordingly.

Our day for inoculation arrived, a bitter cold morning with a strong wind and sleet blowing in from the sea. Forming up before our billet we turned up our collars about our ears and snuggled in to await the arrival of Sgt-Major.

"All present and correct Sgt-Major" said our Sergeant as Bill arrived complete with his regimental cane beneath his arm and as usual standing head and shoulders above us all. He looked us over and then in a kindly voice said:

"Come lads, turn those collars down. We can't have soldiers walking about with their collars up, can we? Let's look smart even if we are frozen stiff."

Silently we all agreed and followed our leader along the cliff top to Prideaux Hospital. That wind took one's breath away. By the time we reached our destination my ears and right cheek were frozen and I was not the only sufferer, as witnessed by the massaging going on as we fell out in front of the hospital. We joined the queue for the jab-'in and out quick' like bayonet practice and move on to make way for the next victim.

What that needle contained I never found out but it flattened the company. Sleeping on the floor was bad enough with a draught from the sea but added to the effects of the inoculation, it was a bit too much. It was true to say that many were 'out for the count' next morning. A sorry sight, men vomiting and others were groaning in what seemed agonies of despair and myself little better than the rest. The only one unaffected seemed to be Pratt, probably his sea-going life had hardened him to such events. He was up and about serving breakfast to the invalids still wrapped in blankets.

"Any breakfast, Cookie? I'll bring it for you."

"What is it Ted?" I asked with visions of some nice toast such as Mother used to make.

"Kippers" he replied.

"No thanks Ted. I think I'll just continue to die." At least that is what I felt like saying and probably did.

Whatever disease that inoculation was supposed to protect us from I never knew but could have been no worse than our sufferings I'm sure. Later such treatments never had the same effect and I was to have many. Sgt-Major Hodgson looked in with Sgt. Pearson and saw our plight.

"Let the lads lie in today Sergeant. They are not fit for parades. I'll see the CO and get them excused."...Good old Bill...what a man!

The weather in March and early April was very cold, nothing wasted it was used for toughening. No excuse for bad weather, work went on as usual. Paddling parade usually straight after breakfast, when feet were immersed in the cold North Sea and no time for them to thaw out before we got boots on again, no dodging, this had to be done. The agony we suffered we little knew was child's play compared to what lay before us in days to come. Those were happy days-not a care in the world. All for a shilling a day!

The company made a name for itself by its singing on the march. No other company had a song leader to compare with our tall Irishman O'Hara with just the voice and the spirit for the job. We swung along to his leadership of 'Tipperary', 'Sons of the Sea', 'Hold your hand out naughty boy' and a host of popular songs of the day together with some of his own compositions based on hymn tunes, with words never intended for Sunday School. We all enjoyed it, as did the good people of Whitley Bay, who stood and watched as we passed by with many a friendly wave and smile. Our Officers had the good sense to see the value of this and O'Hara was always in the front rank on the march, even though there were times when they were the butt of his wit by an impromptu song. "A little child shall lead them" must have been very embarrassing to a newly commissioned young officer as was "O you beautiful doll" to some smart young lady we passed on our way, but I think she would be flattered and certainly it was all in good spirit.

"The Farmer's Boy" was always reserved until we passed a ploughman cutting his lonely furrow and often he would acknowledge our song with a friendly wave. It was unanimously agreed that O'Hara's lance-corporal's stripe was well earned, the first promotion from our ranks.

The psychology of the staff at Whitley Bay was good. We worked hard but they kept us happy. We respected our seniors, their discipline was strict but fair. Only one NCO defaulted and must have regretted it by what happened. The Physical Training Instructor was a man of steel with a body of springs, a specialist in muscular exercises and he expected us to be the same. There was no 'stand easy' with him, we had to do it all. His greatest fault was his tongue, which stung more than the pains we suffered from limbs not yet fit for super gymnastics.

The squad was under his instruction and suffering as usual but trying hard. For once his tongue picked out the wrong man-a quite inoffensive fellow but one who would never make a gymnast, plain to see. Imagine the surprise of the instructor when he left the ranks without a 'by your leave' and marched straight over to the Regimental Sgt-Major standing on parade with the Colonel himself. They were some distance away and Colonel Friend must have sensed something wrong as he allowed the man to speak to him without permission, a thing we all knew just was not done.

"Sir" he said "I wish to complain of the Sergeant's language to me. I have no objection to some words but I am not a bastard and I'm not accepting that title from anyone, not even a Sergeant."

"Sergeant Wright" bawled out the RSM immediately and there and then the instructor got the ticking off of his life in front of us all. We could see him wilt beneath the lash of the RSM's words. Our friend returned to the ranks-honour satisfied and future parades heard sweeter words and probably harder drill. This could not happen in many battalions but illustrates the good sense of our senior officers. After all we were still recruits and volunteers.

Before we left Whitley Bay we had a taste of camp life. In fact we built the camp completely from scratch on virgin soil, pitching sufficient tents to hold the whole battalion. We mastered the art of pitching a tent eventually, at least we got them up but I never saw a tent go up without an argument in all my army days. The technique had something to do with placing the guide rope first. These were fastened to four red pegs placed in the corners of a square, after which the pole was inserted and up she goes, or should I say should go. Like the fitting of puttees there always seemed to be too much material and to have a tent collapse in the middle of the night due to bad fitting was no joke-it happened at times. Similarly there was the need to avoid touching the canvas in wet weather, not always achieved.

At times there were twenty men to a bell tent, all lying with feet to the centre pole and the last man had to fasten the door flaps. Woe betides the man who had to get up in the night to answer nature's call. A boot sufficed for a necessary article providing it wasn't one's own boot. Twenty rifles fastened round the pole could cause havoc if they came adrift and they did, also serving as a convenient rack for sundry caps and equipment.

Camp life was good, as we were favoured with the weather. On probably the coldest night when a Zeppelin airship passed over the camp, we turned out promptly on the alarm and fled to the four corners of the field. Orders were that there must be no delay as we rehearsed in daylight, but this was night and it really was a Zeppelin. Most of us found ourselves in shirt and underpants alone shivering on the very damp grass. Bell tents could be a very easy target in moonlight. No camouflage had yet been thought of and it was a long time before it dawned on the powers that be. The French led the way, hence the name camouflage. We heard next day that the Zeppelin had dropped one bomb on South Shields. It fell on a fair ground and shattered a roundabout. Casualties were nil. So much for the dreaded Zeppelin!

The main parade of the day here was the early morning Regimental Sergeant Major's Parade when he exercised the full battalion for about an hour. This to me was always enjoyed although it took some preparing for if one was to miss his eagle eye. Perish the man who had a button loose or had not shaved before parade or moved in the ranks unless ordered to stand at ease. Even then one waited for his 'easy' before relaxing cramped limbs. All officers attended too, but were mounted. Officers came in for no less scrutiny than we lesser mortals did, one being told to get his hair cut and another to wash the back of his neck. All moved to absolute precision and the arms drill had to be Guard's standard if we would reach it with so short a training. I was never fortunate enough to be right hand man in the front rank when I would have had to take the regulation steps forward and in five drill movements give the time to all to fix bayonets. I felt I could have done it much better than some I saw. Such was my opinion, whether it would have been so was never tested for many months and then on lesser parades.

One evening two of us were leaving camp on our free evening. Seeing the RSM standing near the gate, smartly turned out in his uniform complete with silver-headed cane beneath his arm, we debated whether to salute him or not. As far as we knew he ranked as an officer so we duly gave him our right hand salute, only to be called back by him. On approaching with fear in our hearts, he said quite kindly:

"No, you don't salute me, boys, I'm only a Warrant Officer. You salute an officer who is Commissioned and always bear in mind you are saluting his rank, not the man...Carry on boys, have a good evening out and don't get into trouble."

"Thank you, Sir" I said and doing a smart about turn we marched off. We were learning by degrees. I don't think I ever met another RSM who would have been so considerate to two recruits as he was and it raised him in our esteem as many things did amongst the staff in that camp. Our training went on –field tactics, lectures and musketry, assault courses and long route marches, often behind the excellent Military Band. If anyone did not enjoy it he should not have been there. Strenuous, yes, I completely wore out two pairs of army boots but gained confidence in myself as I did.

As I look back, I reflect that there was always good discipline flavoured with a kind consideration seldom met later. Kit inspection by the CO with our kits laid out in precision in front of the tents, was a lesson in itself. Everything was in line throughout the camp, even to a taut piece of string. Nothing must be out of place (even today I put cutlery away in the same order-knife, fork, spoon etc. as we used to lay out our holdalls). On one occasion we had kits inspected by the CO and RSM who after passing along the line with a comment here and there, returned with the order that all men should doff their tunics. Reaching me, I was ordered to 'about turn' to reveal that one back trouser button was supplanted with a safety pin!

"A lot of responsibility rests on that pin soldier" the Colonel said, "See that it is replaced by a button immediately after parade." It ended there but at later parades in my career it could have led to detention, being confined to barracks.

Early in July the staff had reason to be proud of us as they wished us 'Goodbye', having already told us we were set for transfer as battle reinforcements to regiments in France. Not as a complete unit as would happen to new battalions raised under Kitchener (later known as Kitchener's army), but to several units. It meant for me that along with some 300 men I was transferred to the Northumberland Fusiliers-'The Fighting Fifth' with a motto 'Quo Fata Vocant' being interpreted 'Whither Fate Leads' which I accepted with good faith and became a Fusilier with pride.

There was urgency in our training apparently, for others took another year before going overseas but there was good sense in what happened and later we completed the training we lacked under men with true battle experience on the field.

CHAPTER THREE

FULLY EQUIPPED,
INTO BATTLE

Returning from a few days 'overseas leave' we paraded not knowing just why. Three hundred men were numbered off and the rest dismissed like cutting cheese. No discrimination, if you were in the three hundred that was enough. 'Stand fast and await orders.'

Now we learnt that the Northumberland Fusiliers needed us for their 1st and 2nd Battalions their depot being at East Bolden near Sunderland. It sounded good to me for I was a 'Geordie' by birth having been born at Trimdon, County Durham where my ancestors belonged. The North was anywhere north of the Tees to the family at home and whilst I had every respect for the West Yorkshire Regiment, I welcomed the change.

The fitting went on at speed, full web equipment, khaki overcoats at last in place of Kitchener's blue for home service only and new boots.

Field dressings were to be sewn inside tunics, and with kit bags discarded we learnt to pack everything into a valise and haversack. Only careful folding would enable one to get all in neatly but we did it, always with the reminder to travel lightly.

"You may have to march a long way" said Sgt. Pearson who was genuinely sorry to see us go.

Ammunition pouches were filled with live ammo. for the first time adding to the weight considerably, 150 rounds and an additional 100 in cotton bandoliers slung across the shoulders...but no rifles! So far I had no rifle to call my own, they were collected from time to time for use by other platoons due to a shortage. Probably the extra 100 rounds were to compensate for the weight, also to use us as transport of much needed ammunition elsewhere.

The full Regimental Band led us to Newcastle station where we entrained. The good people of Whitley Bay turned out to see us off standing by the kerbs, some with tears in their eyes as they said good-bye to friends amongst us and we reflected that these people had been our friends.

Colonel Friend and his Officers accompanied us and respect was shown on both sides, we to a team of men admired and they to a body of men who after only three months had learned a lot and made a good show. The band played the regimental march 'God bless the Prince of Wales' as the train moved out, cheers died away and we learnt that Southampton was our destination. We were spared the sight of East Boldon for the time being!

The crossing to Le Havre on a crowded troopship was pleasant as we sat about on deck. 'Housey-housey' games with cries of 'Kelly's eye' (no 1), 'Clickety-click' (no 66), 'Dinky-do' (no 22) and a new one to me 'Fusiliers' (no 5). It was the only game of gambling allowed in the army but card games and Crown and Anchor thrived surreptitiously. Not being a gambler myself, I looked on with interest. I had the good fortune to make the best friend ever in my army days as I chatted with a fellow recruit, one of the three hundred from Whitley Bay. We had similar tastes in reading, recreation and thought. He had been a trainee bank clerk in Bradford, obviously from a good family, well-spoken and no mean scholar but most of all a charming smile and kindly personality. Syd Jowett became my friend and we determined to keep together as far as possible and succeeded in this when we reached our ultimate destination. I introduced him to Platt and others of my acquaintances and we all eventually joined the same platoon in 'X' Company, 1st Northumberland Fusiliers.

Whilst I had many friends and more still to meet, as I look back there was no other like Syd Jowett. My memories of him are of a young man with nothing mean in his nature, a perfect gentleman and ultimately a great soldier.

Eventually we entrained at Rouen for an unknown destination, our first experience of French railways and were not impressed. We did however travel in carriages marked 'Deuxieme Classe' but there was little comfort in that and the speed of the train was such that we actually got off to pick blackberries then jumped on further back as the train moved slowly along. Bolder spirits climbed to the roof and basked in the sunshine with a quick scatter as we approached a tunnel or a bridge. The journey took many hours through the night and into the next day, for a journey I have since done in about three hours. Time dragged on, the card players were reduced to playing for matches whilst we talked and told the tale. Altogether it was not a bad journey but for the sheer monotony of sitting in a carriage eating only what we had brought, now reduced to hard biscuits with a 'mashing' of tea made from water obtained from the engine exhaust when the train made one of its numerous stops. This had its humour too, for it depended how much pressure the obliging driver gave us when he released the valve. The high-pressure steam often blew the tealeaves out of the can and one was left with a small amount of condensed water with a semblance of a brew.

An old soldier returning to the front after a period in hospital said to me:

"You should start smoking lad, it passes the time and you will have a lot of this sort of thing to come, time to whittle away."

So far I had never been a smoker having no intention or inclination for the habit. Perhaps there was something in what I was told so I replied:

"If I do it will be with a pipe. I am sick of seeing you fellows scrounging fags, even tab ends. To me it is a disgusting habit."

Reaching into his pack, Paddy Ecrett, for that was his name, brought out a nice looking briar pipe and gave it to me. Handling it I asked where he had got it for obviously it had been used.

"It's not new" he told me. He had got it from a dead man's pocket. "But it's quite clean, I've burned it out with a hot, red-hot hatpin so all germs must be dead too"

Then from several quarters came gifts of pipe tobacco, issue stuff not fit for cigarette making and not too good even for a pipe. So I began a habit which has followed me all my days since and truth to tell Paddy was quite right it was a comfort and solace in times of monotomy and stress.

Paddy was to become one of our friends in days to come. He was a very likeable Irishman full of unconscious wit. On a later occasion he had a letter and he sat with it in his hands opened for a few minutes then said:

"That's funny, I got this letter addressed to me and there is nothing in it but an empty piece of paper, no writing on it."

"Oh, what will you do with it, Paddy?" I asked.

"Well" he said with a twinkle in his eye "I'll just keep it and answer it sometime."

Some weeks later he was chopping firewood in a trench as we cooked a meal, talking all the time. Suddenly there was a yell and he was swinging his arm round like a windmill and crying:

"I'd sooner have been shot, I'd sooner have been shot. This is a self inflicted wound and a disgrace to a soldier like me."

We found he had chopped his trigger finger off and we sent him off to the dressing station complaining all the time at his misfortune and 'him a regular soldier with 8 years with the colours and 3 on reserve'. Someone found the finger and hurried after him to see if the doctor could put it back for him.

So we lost Paddy for a while but he came back and soldiered on with us again.

CHAPTER FOUR

MEN, HORSES, MUD AND STEW

Poperinghe, a small town in Flanders, to become known to thousands of British soldiers, was a place of feverish activity as we first saw it. Horse transport loaded here with everything an army might need, from the railhead to a background of distant artillery fire in the direction of Ypres. In some respects one might compare the scene with that of a Western film, with horsemen everywhere one looked. A tough band of men with a tougher crowd of mules, which we avoided as much as possible.

We had little time to browse or wander as the reception committee was here to meet us under the Regimental Police Sergeant who gathered us into line and with little delay led us through the town on to a road. There we competed with the overflowing transport for a foothold on the worst road I had seen so far. Mud caked to what became known as fascines (bundles of bracken and twigs tied with steel wire) seemed to be the only way the French knew of making a road. One had to cling to this or run the danger of being precipitated into the deep ditch on each side. One good feature was the picturesque line of poplar trees on either side, which ran for miles. We saw one or two civilians mostly old people dragging their feet to some farm cottage, which looked equally old and decrepit. They evidently had no interest in us but why should they, as we had probably disturbed their once peaceful way of life.

There was no mistaking the direction of the front line as the constant boom of guns reverberated, rising and falling in different directions and above us. Occasionally there was the stutter of a machine gun as aeroplanes met in combat or attempted to evade the thousands of anti-aircraft shells bursting around them. The whine of a shell passed over our heads but was ignored as the column of men and horses plodded along. We reached what was once a village, now merely a row of mud-bespattered houses lining the road. This was Ouerdam where our battalion had its temporary base on a rising ground. A frail wooden bridge reached the camp for vehicles and a plank for pedestrians over a stream of muddy water. This was now a camp for men belonging to the HQ staff and transport who were away in the front line. Horses were tethered to a long line of rope and were placidly eating hay scattered on the ground. There was no cover at all. A few bell tents and a small marquee housed the Quarter Master and his staff. We were shown some bivouacs improvised from blankets strung along between poles.

Perhaps it was because of their unattractive appearance as a home that Syd and I found ourselves unable to be accommodated. Others had already crawled in and it was 'House full'. Left to our own resources, we scrounged about until we found a large packing case amongst the litter in the field, once evidently containing bacon but promising some shelter of a kind.

Two field kitchens with attendants were brewing up tea, which seemed to combine itself with stew and a strong flavour of onions. As we were also served stew we surmised that there could only be a few dixies and once the stew was served the tea followed immediately into the same utensils after a mere lick with a greasy cloth. As we had been told many times 'We're in the army now' so stew and tea was consumed with relish. Bully beef, or corned beef to be precise, is quite good to eat but it can become monotonous and when stewed to shreds as this was, together with dried vegetables and chestnuts, it is a dish one must acquire a taste for. One good item on our menu was the bread, pure white and well baked into two-pound cottage loaves.

The bakers at the base camps somewhere far behind never let us down on quality, although quantity suffered at times due to circumstances beyond their control. A pound a day was supposed to be our ration and by and large we got it.

The gas masks were issued as a prior need. They were simply a piece of black gauze wrapped round a pad of wool impregnated with some chemical substance. Instructions were that on the alarm being given we were to wrap it round mouth and nostrils and should the pad become dry this could be rectified by urinating on it. Someone hearing the usual 'Any questions?' asked if we could not be supplied with maiden water as he thought it would be sweeter. This bright suggestion was met with a laugh. Our humourists had not so far been quenched by our prospects.

Best of all, at long last we were each given a rifle. We'd waited long enough but now I had my very own, number 6668943. Could I ever forget? It was impressed on us that the number was all-important, as we were responsible for our own weapons. When asked, "What is your rifle for?" there is only one answer "To kill the enemy with." Secretly we added, "to defend myself" but never aloud. It must never leave you, always be to hand, and even by your side as you slept. It became part of me and never an encumbrance-one felt naked without it at times. Woe betides the fellow who got one with a sweaty barrel as some did, to be plagued with it on every inspection. Luckily mine was an excellent weapon and I kept it for months. I could recognise that rifle in pitch darkness and was never known to pick up the wrong one, nor should one ever accept a rifle where the number on bolt and barrel did not agree. This was disastrous, not only that the bolt might jam but also it would be assumed that you had been careless. I've seen it happen but not to me. Later I learned more. My training was still in its infancy.

That first night in Ouerdam, Syd and I took refuge in our bacon box some 4x3x4 feet, squeezing in to escape the rain which had been saving itself for our particular baptism. Our sleep, if any, was relieved occasionally as we got out to take the cramp out of our limbs and backs, or as Syd said, "to get a rest." A grey wet dawn saw the transport making its way back from the line having delivered vital supplies under cover of darkness. The never-ending procession of horses, mules and men now weary and muddy, passed with the added rumble of motor lorries and gun tractors. To stand and watch as we did that day was also an education in language. Artillery drivers who rode astride, seemed to have the richest collection of profane words of all and when I later saw them at work I forgave them all. As we looked on, we saw men who had recently been shop assistants, clerks, tinkers, tailors and all, with here and there men who wore the ribbons of other campaigns. Later we knew them as our closest friends.

We took the road at dusk bound to join our battalion in the line at St.Eloi. Setting off in sections of four, we soon gave way to the transport, which spattered us with mud, as we took the same road. As darkness covered us we crossed open country to reach a communication trench meandering away into the direction of a display of blazing Verey lights and shellbursts. Reaching Dickebusch we halted and noticed the signs of 'Boulangerie', 'Estaminet', 'Chocolat' and 'Café' but all were now closed for the night. The occupants were asleep, still hanging on in a village where bullets and shells threaten their existence. New loads were added to our already heavy equipment, with rations in two sandbags to a man or a coil of barbed wire, horrible stuff, ammunition boxes one box to two men, very heavy, or a duckboard to add to the millions already doing service forward. We passed a small hut with a stretcher lying outside with a man on it, completely covered with a grey blanket.

"Wilf, dead! This is war." Syd whispered, as orders were against talking, enemy ears were listening. Along the communication trench we came to a junction where a Sergeant Major stood.

"First twenty men to the right" he said and we turned right:

"Quo Fata Vocant." What simple things assume importance. We were going to the second line in reserve, the twenty to the front line – some for the first and last time. As the night brought heavy bombardment of trench mortars on them, several of our late friends were killed. By sheer chance we had escaped. I particularly grieved for a fellow named Rice, the brother of a famous professional boxer serving in the York and Lancs. My letter to my brother Jack was the first intimation of his death. I remember Rice as a man whom when preparing for bed in a tent with us, had around his neck a long string of beads.

"Ricey, what are you wearing those things for?" someone asked.

Without any embarrassment he replied that they were his rosary, given to him by his Mother when he left home, to wear always for his salvation. His Catholic faith meant everything to him and, I know gave him comfort at the very end. Syd and I had a great regard for him even before we knew this. He was a most likeable young man who would have been an excellent soldier. He lost his life through a foolish action of a young officer who had placed a placard the day before for the Germans to read with the caption 'Gott strafe der Kaiser'. If he thought it was funny, he would have also learned that joking with Fritz is a dangerous practice. His banner went up in flames and men with it. This incident was never reported in the Regimental Magazine or in its history but it was a fact we all knew.

In the morning we moved forward to take our places in the front line via the communication trench, where we learned to move quickly at points where the parapet was low. To linger was to become the target of the wily snipers just waiting for the slightest sign of movement before letting fly with deadly aim.

So far Syd and I had only met a few of the famous first battalion and looked forward to meeting the core of the unit, the actual rank and file who bore the brunt of the fighting, not those who worked behind the lines sending up supplies. Of all the places we were to visit St. Eloi stands out as the most memorable. The trenches as we saw them that day were in good condition, although the word trench is a misnomer. In reality they were formed by heavy breastworks of neatly piled sandbags, laid with precision, some ten to twelve feet thick to the parapet, facing the enemy and the parados in the opposite direction somewhat lower and less in depth. It takes at least 6 feet of earth-filled sandbags to stop a rifle bullet at close range i.e. 600yards or less. Shellfire of course would play havoc with parapets but still one had the protection of them until finally demolished.

Our arrival was welcomed by all as we moved along, being distributed to various platoons and sections during our progress. Syd and I kept together and had the good fortune to be posted to a section of No 2 platoon X Company under an able Sergeant Newsome another ex-regular army and an old fusilier. He lost no time in initiating us into our duties with his words:

"This is the front line, the enemy are in front of you. This is a long distance as things are, generally others you will see are much closer, down to a few yards in fact. Whilst you are here you will never take off any clothing or equipment at any time. You will always keep your rifle loaded and close to hand, ready for use immediately, and you never sleep. Any questions?"

"How long are we here for, Sergeant?" someone asked.

"Well we do not know but some say seven days"

"But you said we never sleep, Sergeant" our spokesman said. "Surely we can't keep awake for seven days!"

Newsome smiled "Well lads, what I mean is, there is no time allotted for sleep, duty first and sleep as you can find time and place, providing you do not endanger the position. You will learn as you go along. It works out somehow."

Then we were posted to sentry duty, two men to a bay, for the trench is split into bays with barricades at intersections to protect from explosives falling into the trench. Warnings were given as to what to do and not to do. First, do not expose yourself above the parapet in daylight except for the briefest second. Enemy snipers were forever on the lookout for the slightest target and they were crack shots. This we soon learned as I was provided with a periscope which was a piece of mirror on a stick, about 4x2inches square. This I held up for observation of the enemy lines, with the remark from Newsome that I should not even leave that exposed for long as it would get smashed.

"At 600 yards Sergeant, never" I said, then came the whizz of a bullet over my head.

"I told you" Sergeant said. "Well, he can hit it now" and I slowly waved it to and fro to make a moving target. Crash! And I was left with a piece of stick in my hand, mirror gone and a look of amazement on my face.

"So I've lost a periscope now" Newsome said "and I haven't got another but never mind it was a good lesson, better than anything I could say" and he smiled. I was forgiven.

The day went on more or less quietly, gunfire and the stutter of a machine gun and the occasional 'phut' as a bullet buried itself into our parapet. We were introduced to the making of tea over a fire without smoke. This was an art in itself, one procured wood from wherever it could be found, a broken duckboard was a godsend as we splintered it into pieces like matchsticks and with a piece of old letter started a small fire on the fire-step.

Meanwhile one's companion sat with his cap in his hand to disperse by fanning any little smoke which may be made. The mess tin held the water from our water bottles, precious liquid this, and we finally reached boiling point. In went a handful of tea and presto! We had a brew never equalled anywhere and the mainstay of the British Tommy. We were thankful that of all things tea was usually in good supply along with sugar and tinned milk.

All opposing forces universally accept 'Stand to'. It is a period of about one hour preceding nightfall and daybreak-the most likely time for an attack to take place, but it served another function for us. We ceased any work that was not vital and 'stood to arms'. No one was excepted-officers, medical staff, signallers, and the lot. Syd and I enjoyed this period as we usually shared it with some particular friends and it was a time for chatter. Someone to talk to of home or tell a story, humorous or sombre, tales of other days in the lines and many tips to add to what we had already gleaned.

Syd's introduction to the 'Geordies' was a revelation to him, speaking always perfectly good English with a Grammar School background; their brogue must have been 'double Dutch' to him at first. For myself it came easily, for my father and mother had retained much of it themselves, and my early years were in the North. These men we were to spend so long with, were mainly ex-regular soldiers called up with the reserve or Militia, some already with several years as regulars. The battalion had been in France since 1914 and had taken part in the retreat from Mons, The Marne, Neuve Chappelle and other battles. They were in fact the remnant of the thin red line and still it was thin, as witnessed by the length of time we had to do before being relieved as we held our positions in the trenches. Many were ex-miners, tough, hardworking, but good friends and one felt a security with such men at one's side. Their gaiety was unquestioned and their dialect added to many a tale.

I was accepted more or less immediately but Syd was an enigma, for his cultured voice gave them the impression that he was a man, but they liked him and the liking increased on both sides. One phrase amused us all, whereas speech is sometimes punctuated by words such as "You know", "Like." Syd's was often "It's all very fine and large" continuing perhaps with "You fellows may think as you like but my opinion is..." and all would sit spellbound as he gave us his shafts of wit or knowledge on some situation or idea. He was accepted as a 'canny lad' and many came to him later to advise them on some problem or help to write a letter. He never failed to help.

Here we were to meet our new Company Sergeant-Major Drayson. Unlike our old friend CSM Hodgson, he was small, neat and light-footed. A long-serving soldier, he gave me the impression that in any rank he would be happy so long as he was 'soldiering'. He was always ready to talk freely with his men and enjoy a joke with them. To his men he was known as 'Cock Drayson' and this was in no sense derogatory. He was 'Cock' to us all and although not a Geordie he knew their idiosyncrasies to a 'T'. This narrative will tell more of him but here I must make a footnote. A recent visit to the Regimental Museum at Alnwick Castle revealed a plaque, framed along with his medals and to inform me for the first time that he died in action. The curator was good enough to send me the footnote below, for which I am grateful.

St George's Gazette, 31st July 1918.
"*RSM John Drayson, MC, was born at Willsborough, Kent, in 1888. He enlisted into the Fifth Fusiliers in 1906 and served with them in India from 1906 to 1913, during which time he earned the Mohmand Expedition Medal, in 1912. He came to Portsmouth with the Battalion in 1913, and with them went out to France with the 'Old Contemptible' Army in 1914. In the present war he was three times mentioned in despatches and was awarded the Military Cross in 1917, being personally decorated by the hand of HM the King in September of that year. He was killed in action on the tenth of June and his loss will be keenly felt by all who knew him. He was a gallant man and a good soldier. To his widow we offer our deepest sympathy in her loss.*"

The following incident reveals how likeable he was.

Our first night in the front line Syd and I were posted to do sentry duty in the same bay with instructions to keep a good look out and fire at any target we could find, particularly anyone approaching the barbed wire in front. In our enthusiasm we did just that, except no one approached, but there were plenty of flashes from enemy rifles and bullets from them could hit someone. The duty lasted almost to dawn. Other men had other duties, ration carrying, parapet repairs, etc.

Following 'Stand to' in the morning the Sgt-Major came along with two men carrying an ammunition box to replenish rounds fired during the night.

"How many do you want?" I heard him say to each man.

"Fifty Sir." "Twenty Sir", "None Sir" and so on until he came to me. My reply of "Two hundred and fifty Sir" sent him into a roar of laughter.

"And what would you have done if the Germans had attacked us in the last hour or so?" he asked me, still laughing. It had never occurred to me.

"You'll learn" he said, "Don't do it again. I hope some of the bullets killed a German. You never know, men have been killed by stray bullets before this." And he moved on, still laughing.

Newsome had another word with me in the same vein, but they had both let me down lightly in such a jolly way. I felt no embarrassment, whereas anyone else but a man like 'Cock' Drayson would have given me a real rocket. 'Cock' was his nickname to us but never in his hearing of course. We were fortunate to have our baptism of fire under men like him and Newsome.

A pint of water a day does not go far. Here we had an addition from a little brook, which meandered, across No-man's land through our trench. There was a notice stuck in it 'POISON' in large letters. It was obvious why-it came from enemy lines. This little brook, like the brook Kidron in the Bible, never failed to supply us with sweet water which we boiled well just in case. No one ever suffered at our side, nor I supposed did the Germans who most likely drank it too. Good clear brooks are rare in Flanders.

Of water we were to see much. The rainfall in Flanders is considerable and the ground holds it near the surface. One only has to dig some two feet in this region to strike water, hence the breast works and trenches dug below the water level are only tenable with any comfort by the use of duckboards, of which the Pioneers supplied us by the million.

Sgt. Newsome was not wrong when he said we were here for seven days or more and that was after they had already done some days before we arrived. This gave us time to become acclimatised and to get to know our new friends better still. There was good sense in placing new men with old seasoned troops, whereas the Battalions which came out later as full units had to find their own way. Home training, no matter how good, did not give any real training in trench warfare, the building of good barricades or dugouts. Nor did it teach how to take cover under the sudden arrival of a trench mortar, rifle grenade or that infantry man's particular foe, the whizz-bang, an 88mm shell fired at great velocity to any target no matter how small, even down to one man at a time. The shell arrived, burst somewhere near, if not on the parapet with a resounding crack, and then you heard the gun, for they were not far distant. They were the equivalent of our own 18-Pounders, which were to our rear and ready at all times but with less ammunition than Jerry had. We waited for some retaliation from our own batteries but seldom did it come for they were limited to so many rounds a day, such was the shortage in 1915.

Sir Winston Churchill, then Major Churchill, said on January 6th 1915:

"The sound and accepted principle of military organisation is undoubtedly that new army units be placed with seasoned troops."

This was also Field Marshall Sir Douglas Haig's belief but Kitchener, then Secretary of State for War, overrode him. He advised that the new army should be trained and sent into action as complete units, which proved disastrous. (Quoted from "Douglas Haig – the educated soldier" by John Terraine).

So to return to our new friends a word picture must suffice: Jackie Forrest, perhaps to be our greatest friend in the early days had many years of soldiering to his credit. He lacked nothing in his abilities in the field or on parade doing ceremonial drill. He had a strong Northumbrian accent. If you visit Bamburgh Castle or Alnwick today and note how the guides burr their R's making Forest 'Fowest', trench 'twench' and so on. He cannot possibly overcome this fault if he is a true Northumbrian. It has survived the ages and he will keep it to his dying day. My brother Arthur had it handed down genetically. At school he was often taken to task for it and had the indignity to have to stand up before the class to sound 'rrr' but never once did it succeed. It has some relation to the formation of the tongue and is a true North Country trait.

Jackie first met us wearing a thick black beard. No razor had touched him for several days and he had to shave twice a day to keep reasonably clean as a soldier should. How he shaved with the piece of tin we were given, I never solved but I do know that he frequently applied for a new one saying that his old one had been lost or worn out 'in the exigencies of the service'. How he got the word exigencies was a wonder for the Geordie had a happy knack of reconstructing long words into something to suit himself. The communication trench was always the 'cumication twench', his rifle was his 'wifle' and 'come on' was always 'howay lad'.

Jackie was an artist with a pick or shovel. My first attempts made him laugh,

"Nay lad tha' handles it like a spyon. Watch me, thu' gans like this" and in went his spade to its full depth and he lifted the equivalent of Flanders soil to three of my 'spyunfuls'. Likewise my handling of a pick was a terror to behold but I was determined to equal them some day and eventually I gained some proficiency.

We found Jackie the scrounger par excellence. If we were short of anything –ask Jackie! Be it tea, meat, bread or a piece of equipment, Jackie would find it. He was adept at stealing chickens too, as a later story will tell. We learned to 'win' things ourselves when necessary. If someone was foolish enough to leave something unguarded he deserved to lose it that was the maxim and few ever complained but some things were sacrosanct. No one ever took a bayonet or a rifle that was not his own. The code of honour forbade this. Jackie had no fear. He was a tower of strength in tight corners and nothing seemed to please him more than a night patrol into enemy lines. His cousin Hughie Campbell served alongside him in our platoon. Hughie was a smaller man, also a regular and equally likeable. He had a twin brother who also served with him and they had been inseparable until June 14th when he was killed going forward under fire at Bulleward Farm at Hooge. It was said they were hand in hand as the brother fell but Hughie soldiered on. This engagement was the reason for our re-inforcing the battalion as their casualties had been very heavy but they earned battle honours, now decorating the Colours. He had no enemies, liked by all for his humour and unfailing strength. These are two of the band of men I shall refer to, gone now but will we ever see their like again?

Rations came up at night packed in sandbags. Distribution was for each bag to be divided between four or six men according to supplies. This could vary too, when some had been lost in transport or our casualties left us with the rations of those we had lost. Bread, jam (usually plum and apple or apricot, seldom strawberry which was most likely purloined by those who handled it before we did at some distant base depot), tinned milk, butter in tins, the inevitable Corned Beef (bully), cheese and dried fruit, with occasionally some other tit-bit. Tea and sugar were always adequate and there was usually a surplus –a sandbag half full of tea and sugar mixed which was carried in addition to our normal load of equipment. It was common property and we took turns in carrying it. The army biscuits were as near to dog biscuits as makes no matter. They supplemented the bread, which was normally a pound of bread per man.

We later found the biscuits made good fuel and many a tin burned as charcoal.

It was necessary for us to have 'mucking-in pals' i.e. those who shared in the dividing of the ration bag, especially the tin of jam, butter and the brewing of tea. 'Mucking-in' was the general term but to the Geordie he had his 'Marrer', a term from mining days when men worked together on the coalface. Syd and I soon had some good 'marrers' and shared many a happy though frugal meal.

'Geordie' Summers was another we met at St. Eloi who is worth a mention. He was 'marrer' to Hughie and Jackie and was even broader in his speech. Later we were billeted in a barn. Night had fallen and we lay on the straw going to sleep with the sentry outside keeping vigil, when we heard the sound of approaching feet.

"Halt! Wheeze that?" Geordie Summers challenged.

"Orderly Officer" came the reply in a cultured voice. He was doing his rounds.

"Advance Orderly Officer and gi'e the counterpane" Geordie cried in a loud voice.

" Counterpane" Syd said to me. "What's he talking about? It's countersign, a counterpane is bedding" and then I heard him chuckling as he snuggled down to rest.

'P' trenches at St. Eloi had other dangers besides whizz-bangs, for under our feet there were sounds of tunnelling and we walked with light tread lest we gave away our exact position. We had already felt reverberations of mines exploded in neighbouring trenches and we trusted that luck would see us away before Jerry turned his attentions on us. Our own sappers were working too, tunnelling beneath what was known as the 'Mound of death', a small rise in the enemy's lines, which we surveyed more than we dared for him to know. It was to become the scene of a later battle.

Our days at St. Eloi came to an end and we were relieved at night and made our way back to Dickebusch, there to form up for the trek back to Ouerdam.

The men were weary after 12 days in the line without even the relief of taking off their boots, lack of good sleep and constant vigil. Ranks were ragged but the promise of warmth and better food encouraged us. We were not to be favoured for long, as we learned that we were to spend only one night there before going on to St. Julien, there to relieve another battalion. We made the most of it, fortunately gaining the comfort of a bivouac. Stew appeared again along with tea and a bath. This was a tub of warm water from the field kitchen, placed in the field with only a hessian sheet for privacy and one man at a time in the bath. By the time we reached it the water was almost solid with soapsuds but we made do hastily as others waited for a turn.

We also had a 'snapping parade' for the first time. Lice were added to our discomfort, invading the seams of shirts and pants to breed and feed on our bodies. We learnt that these were universally accepted as one of the exigencies of the service. No one is free of them, as witnessed by the men with shirts and every article of clothing being closely inspected, as the pests were crushed between thumbnails. A change of clothing brought little relief, as apparently the field laundry had not yet found a true killer so what hope had we?

The day passed quickly and night found us on our way through the ruined city of Ypres. (Wipers to some, Yips to the Geordie and Ieper to its inhabitants.) What a place, once a thriving centre of trade with a Cathedral and Cloth Hall from medieval times and surrounded by a wall and moat, now disintegrating beneath almost constant bombardment of enemy guns. We did not linger as we clattered along its roads to our destination, the trenches at Poteje where we relieved the Sherwood Foresters. The trenches were good and dugouts clean and one could almost say every prospect pleased as the sun shone!

This particular part of the Ypres salient was at that time considered 'cushy' or at least not as hard pressed as the tips of the salient near Hooge and St. Eloi. It was to the north of the city of Ypres and Vlamert-inghe. From here we could get a good view of the city and daily we had the unpleasant experience of what sounded like an express train passing over our heads-the 17 inch shells from the German long distance siege guns. The resulting explosion raised a heavy cloud of black smoke and earned the nickname of 'Jack Johnson's' (he being the current heavy-weight boxer). We also had facing us a long line of enemy observation balloons which kept us under surveillance every day. Aeroplanes constantly passed over one way or the other, the enemy planes being in the ascendance. One of ours we dubbed the Mad Major. He flew an old biplane with struts and wire like a huge kite. Speed was not his forte nor height for he could be seen sitting at the controls as he passed very low over us. He was obviously spotting for the guns and seemed to have no regard for the shells. Once he came into sight every German anti-aircraft gun opened up on him. He rocked occasionally but kept his course and returned, probably satisfied with his view of the enemy which was to be a target for his battery.

The salient in front of Ypres became the most well known battlefield of the time. Once countryside of rolling fields and farms, it was now becoming a land of desolation and destruction as we clung to it. Men in their thousands laid down their lives there. 'They shall not pass' seemed to be the watchword and although we held the lower slopes and suffered more for it, we never gave up hope of one day moving forward. Strategy is no part of this narrative although we supposed there were reasons that we knew not so we did our many daily chores. Pick and shovel meant more than rifles. Sandbags were filled by the thousand and we built and built, learning the technique of header and stretcher to perfection.

On one occasion working under Sgt. Newsome with a number of bags to fill which he laid in neat rows higher and higher. One bright spark had the idea of shortening our hours by filling partly with grass. Newsome quickly spotted this and emptied them out saying:

"Some day, someone will stand behind this barricade for shelter and expect to get it. Grass won't do, it must be soil and well packed." There were no more attempts to fool him. The dugouts were good as we knew them but merely shelter from shrapnel. A direct hit would be death to everyone in them. We learned that under shellfire it was best to have a deep trench, not too wide and trust to luck, as we were plagued with whizz-bangs and mortars. The latter were a kind of oil drum filled with high explosives. Once dropped into a trench the damage was terrific.

"Trench mortar right," meant move left and quick but only after it began to descend could one guess where it would fall. Our reply to this was very feeble at the time – only a 60-pounder with a metal head like a football and a steel shank some two feet long. If we had possessed more of them and specially trained squads had operated them they would have been more effective. When in use there was no doubt of their power but what we did not like was when the steel shank came back our way with a whizz and velocity to be feared. It usually led to more retaliation from the enemy, the mortar men having already cleared off to safer quarters.

The trenches had in each bay a rack wedged into the parapet on which hung hand grenades. There were some of metal with long tape tails which exploded on impact, known as 'onions'. I never saw one used but understood they were extremely dangerous to the user, especially from a trench. If one hit the back of the trench when preparing to throw it meant instant death or severe injury. Whilst we were here, they were declared obsolete along with several other models.

Our specialist-bombing corporal loved his trade. He said he had one aim 'The VC or death.' By his antics we guessed which it would be. Deciding that all old bombs, of which there were many, should be disposed of, he had the idea of putting them all into a shell hole behind the trench and blowing them up. For our protection he suggested we place a sniper's plate over them too. With some trepidation, we carried the stuff and laid it in the trench. He supervised the laying of a trail of fuse and his snipers plate half-inch steel about 3ftx2ft on top. We retreated to await results, he standing with us with a satisfied smile, whilst we prepared to duck even further. BANG up it went like a 'Jack Johnson' itself. All went well but that plate took to the air like a buzz saw. It boomeranged round us for minutes until it finally settled in no-man's land. Syd and I said nothing; Jackie and Co. said it for us.

"Did he think he was Chin-ling-soo, the famous conjurer, with his bleeding bombs. He should get the hell out of it and earn his VC somewhere else. Disturbing the peace, he was!" and Corporal or no Corporal he had to take it. A great joke which could have had serious consequences.

Here we saw for the first time the new Mills grenade though still in short supply. This was a great improvement and is still the finest hand grenade. We saw the last of the 'Jampot' which was nicknamed 'Ticklers Artillery' after the maker of the jam once contained in the tins. The early soldiers had made their own bombs with discarded tins by filling them with a little explosive and whatever shrapnel they found and even stones. The fuse was lighted with a match or cigarette end and it was supposed to have a few seconds before it blew up but many failed to explode and some too soon, an altogether unreliable weapon. The Germans with their usual thoroughness had already come prepared from the first with a stick bomb easily carried in the waist belt but not anything like as destructive as the Mills.

Enemy snipers were very busy, visibility being very good, one moved about with care, especially when passing a low parapet. I volunteered to do a little sniping and conceived the idea of going into a ruined house just behind the trench at night, to remain until next day and try out my marksmanship again. Wiser heads prevailed and I had to drop the idea. How wise they were, the next day the remains of the house received a direct hit and I should have gone with it- lucky man!

"I shouldn't have liked to lose you there Cookie" Sgt. Newsome said and I agreed.

The weather was fine and all things considered our eight days here did us good. We managed to sleep and on one occasion Syd and I put in a good eight hours concealed in a comfortable trench, quite dry and lost to the platoon. Our absence had to be explained to Sergeant but he made no bones about it knowing that had anything serious happened, we should have come out without any demur.

With the few hours at Ouerdam, the time in the trenches at St. Eloi and Potije were considered one spell, twenty-one days in all, and the longest so far as was known, for any battalion. This showed the shortage of men and as we learned there the shortage of shells, for our artillery was very quiet. Back to Ouerdam, there to be drilled and mucked about as we saw it. What did we want with arms drill, square bashing, and saluting drill? What had that to do with what we had been doing these last twenty days? The army never lets up; an idle man is a poor soldier, better keep moving. It does him good and he will not get into trouble.

They probably thought the same about money. So far, since coming to join the Expeditionary Force I had no pay. At Ouerdam at last the table was laid out in the field covered with a blanket and we were told to parade for pay. Well we knew the drill for this, caps on, a smart salute, pick up pay tendered by an officer sitting at the table, another smart salute, about turn, quick march and here we were five francs to the good. Five Francs! Fifty pence in English money, the franc being worth 10d or near enough as far as we knew. Precious little for all that sandbagging alone and the carrying of duckboards etc. The actual soldiering we would give freely as a duty but had we been employed as labourers, which we were for a great part of our time, our pay packet would have bulged. Still we had to find what those five francs could do in Poperinghe or Ouerdam. The good people of Ouerdam looked on us as being millionaires and we found five francs could buy quite a lot if spent carefully. For one thing Syd and I soon found that any house was open house. We could enter with a "Bon jour madam", find a seat near the stove and partake of coffee at 1d a cup. Good coffee, 'avec sucre, du lait' too. The cottages were very primitively furnished with stone flagged floors, a pot-bellied stove standing in the middle of the floor and a coffee pot which never left it except to be refilled with water or new coffee grounds. This was percolated through what seemed to be an old sock attached in some way to the lid containing the coffee. New grounds went in on top of the old until it would hold no more and I seldom saw it emptied. Soon others joined us around the stove to tell the tale and converse with madam and monsieur as best we could. We picked up a little French and Flemish with Syd airing his schoolboy French but not always with success. There was also a universal dish known as 'Pomme de terre Fritz'-fried eggs and chips. Chips with everything. Quite like home!

The Estaminet or boozer we disdained being teetotal but Jackie and Hughie told us we were missing out on the best of things. No one gets drunk here they said, the beer wasn't strong enough and at 1d a glass it was known as a 'penny blob', one hop and a lot of water. The next day we joined the others in a new atmosphere-the local. It was small with a bar little more than a small counter in one corner, with barrel, bottles etc neatly displayed. Madame, Monsieur and an even greater attraction, his buxom daughter were all busy attending to the needs of Les Anglais.

There was beer, 'pomme de terre fritz' and for those who could afford it, wine, Vin Blanc (awful stuff), Vin Rouge, Malaga and Cognac. For those not given to intoxicants, Grenadine which is a kind of syrup. We sampled the beer, not bad to virgin palates, probably good for the bladder and kidneys, Syd thought and we were not likely to be going back to camp singing 'Tipperary' after a few glasses. The cheery company made a very pleasant evening as we scraped our army boots on Madame's stone floor. Someone started a song so we all joined in and for the time being forgot all our troubles. Jackie said he wished he'd brought his 'gew-gaw' which I explained to Syd was a Jew's harp. He had never seen one, a primitive metal instrument, once popular in the North, played whilst gripping it in one's teeth and twanging wires like a pair of bones.

The Redcaps came in to see the place close down, as drinking hours were regulated as at home. We noted there was no fraternisation between them and our friends. Was it that they envied the clean khaki, leather belt complete with revolver and red topped cap, or maybe some previous brush with the law? Our five francs were well spent, even providing some French bread and eggs to supplement tomorrow's breakfast rations.

It was noted that a neighbouring Estaminet supplied the ASC troops, the 'six bob a day' men who did not fraternise with us either. Their songs rang out as we passed, attuned to better stuff than we could afford. Jackie and his friends had noticed something else, the barrels standing in the yard at the back. Later having taken to our 'bivvies' and nearly asleep we were awakened by a call to "come out and get it",'it' being one of the aforementioned barrels, silently transported across the plank footbridge up the slope to our abode. Dixies, mess tins, empty canisters, anything that would hold liquid, was produced.

All had to be cleared before morning, some twenty gallons at least and by daylight not a stave of the barrel remained, all cleared. During the morning the Regimental Quartermaster, our Company QM known to us as 'Jack Canuck', a very conscientious Canadian, and our French interpreter in his blue uniform arrived together with a civilian. They all began peering into bivouacs and round about as if they were seeking the Crown Jewels.

"This gentleman" he said indicating the 'civvy' "has lost a barrel of beer and thinks it was stolen and came to this camp. Do any of you know anything about it?"

He waited for an answer as we stood with innocence personified. Jackie who was always to the fore in such situations said:

"No sor, it isn't heor, ah divent ken how it could be Sor. Neebody could have browt it in wi'out us seeing him Sor." Then added "Have ye tried the Jock's camp, Sor? They likely kna summink."

Sergeants confirmed this and Corporals and our inquisitors departed with "Funny thing" said the QM to the Interpreter. "There is no sign of it here, not even the metal hoops as if they had disposed of the barrel." This was conveyed to Monsieur as he glanced back with suspicion.

"Where did the barrel go Jackie?" I asked him later.

"We cooked the breakfast on it and hoyed the hoops in the beck" adding "By, but that barrel tyuk some getting ower the plank, it was good beer though."

So the incident closed.

Our few days at Ouerdam were coming to an end. Speculations were made as to our next move into the line. Meanwhile, mail had arrived and parcels from home, which were very welcome, especially the home-made cakes, chocolate and sweets, not to mention the Woodbines, always the favourite smoke. Although they were the cheapest (one penny for five when I left home) men would exchange their dearer Gold Flake for the popular 'Woody'. My father always sent me Greys, a very expensive good cigarette which Syd enjoyed whilst I still preferred my pipe. Nothing was wasted of cigarettes here as the smokers had the knack of finishing the tabs completely. We also had some 'chewers', ex-miners who chewed the black twist tobacco and then spat it out with an aim acquired after long practice.

Tim Nugent was the oldest man among us, far too old for this life, but as tough as any. An ex-militia man and miner and a full blooded Geordie. His eyesight was failing and we younger men often looked after him in the line. One night I came by his side and as he stood on sentry duty chewing and spitting towards the German line, with each expecto-ration came the remark:

"Nasty buggers! Bloody Germans! Take that!" as he shot a good plug of thick brown liquid forward. He had not heard or seen me and I remarked:

"Anything wrong Tim?"

"No hinney" he replied "just a nasty taste in me mouth."

What happened to Tim eventually I never knew although he was with us some time. Syd and I liked old Tim. Once out of the line and sent to hospital, he would never come back for sure. He was an old man and looked it. There were others but Tim was nearest to us. He lost a son in the Durham Light Infantry whilst he was with us.

CHAPTER FIVE

DOWN INTO THE WOODS

As we approached the scene of battle and the communication trenches, the old hands told us this was going to be Sanctuary Wood and the prospect was pretty grim from all accounts. Again we passed through Ypres and out by the Menin Gate. At the famous Hell-fire Corner we saw a scene of devastation but nothing to what it would become later. We entered the woods at night with guides taking us to our respective trenches to relieve men who were glad to be going back. Trees were still standing but many had been brought down by shell and mortar fire. The constant noise of rifle fire and the whine of bullets or worse, the ricochet from a branch caused us to keep ducking. Although we knew the bullet that hits a man is never heard approaching, ducking is instinctive and it takes a long time to get out of the habit, if ever.

As we left the dump just outside the wood, we were loaded with the usual extras, barbed wire, ammunition boxes, rations, water and duckboards. These added to our difficulties for here the trenches leading through are in bad shape. "Wire underfoot", "Wire overhead", "Broken duckboard" warned our leaders as we struggled along. We met a party coming the other way and squeezed past with many curses as someone gets a poke in the face with a rifle or a swipe with a duckboard but on we went. At least we had survived one danger, the dump itself. Here in haste and what seemed like confusion, were horses and mounted men giving orders and supplies lying about waiting to be picked up. The enemy knew this spot, as no doubt we knew his and as a few shells can drop here at random, everyone had to be on the lookout. Even the horses and mules knew this, as once their heads turned homeward they needed no bidding. Probably the smell of rotting horseflesh prompted them as it did us. We did not linger, the communication trench felt much safer.

Daylight revealed more of our situation and we noted that the Sergeant, Jackie and Co were on the alert as never before. They knew this place well! Some writers talk of the trees and flowers they saw on active service but not in Sanctuary Wood. Trees there were and probably flowers too but when every tree is a menace, probably hiding a sniper picking one out in his sights, one takes no notice whether it is oak or ash. Apart from ourselves, the only living things we saw were rats. These we had seen before but here they seemed to be bigger, stronger and braver, judging by the way they invaded our dugouts openly and ran the parapet regardless of the danger. Was it that here the food was better for the place stank of putrefaction and dead men.

"Right mate, it's all yours and you are welcome" he said as I took over from the previous sentry. He wasted no time in handing over duties and reports, and just dashed off to join the men we were relieving, looking forward to Ouerdam and its comforts after a few days of this.

"This is a hell of a place," Sergeant Newsome told us "quite different from anything you've seen yet. You'll be lucky if you get any sleep here, as this is probably the worst of the trenches in the wood or all the Salient." Men had returned from hospital after being wounded and there was some re-arrangement of sections. We lost one or two old comrades but gained new ones. One was a full corporal, wearing ribbons showing his service in India and South Africa. He was known as Paddy and was to become a great friend to us all. His Irish brogue added to his charm, as did his wit but this was his element, a tough man in a tough spot. He quickly had us working with him, strengthening the parapet, telling us what the dangers were, what points we had overlooked and a few hints on how to keep a rifle clean and free from mud. One could not guess his age but his medals gave a clue and yet he was as sprightly as the rest of us. He placed every sentry personally, instructing them what to do and what to avoid, even to fixing a sandbag to ensure a better aim and a better foothold on the firestep.

No one took any chances here; the enemy was too close. In fact we hardly knew how close, as the trenches were almost indistinguishable from the undergrowth in the shade of the trees. Only the sound of a rifle revealed the short distance, which was no-man's land, and there was a maze of barbed wire our own touching theirs. If there were any gaps they were only known to the night patrol and that was a job I still had to do.

Paddy took Syd and I under his wing. He was intrigued with Syd, always called him 'Jarrett' and told him that one day he would make a good officer. He often questioned us as to how we came to be here and would have it that we were brothers or if not we must have had the same mother. If ever we were going on a particular duty he wanted to know and made sure we had all we needed as well as his good advice. To move along this trench was to risk death –a low parapet, a sniper's particular spot or a rifle grenade that came without warning often falling right in the trench. He only once lost his temper with me. Continuous shellfire can, strange to say, make one sleepy and I had crept into a small dugout and dropped off to a sound sleep, oblivious to all that was going on around me. During this time the trench received a very heavy shelling and the aim was very close. The parapet went, the dugouts blown in and there was total devastation. They found me in what had been an unused shelter, fast asleep and Paddy made every effort to wake me but to no avail. I was all in. When I did eventually come to and joined them, quite oblivious as to what had happened, I got full force of Paddy's anger. He told me he had even threatened me with a bayonet but never a sound had I made. Then he relaxed and said something about supposing young b....s like me needed more sleep than old men like him. He was glad I was alright and I heard how bad the shelling had been.

This was only one of the strafes we got. If enemy guns were bad so were our own, for not being sure where the trenches were, they often dropped their shells short with devastating effect. The worst came twice a day from one gun of the enemy's which had us in enfilade perfectly. As soon as he opened up we knew what was going to happen. A shell at one end of the trench then he shortened range and followed up bay by bay. There was nothing we could do but evacuate along the bays until it finished, usually averting the shell with a barricade between us. Then one day he was firing faster than ever and we could not move fast enough. Hearing the approach of the shell we dived down into the corner of the bay in a heap as it exploded above us on the parapet. Down came sandbags and there was a general scramble to extricate ourselves. The shelling ceased and we returned to our posts or what was left of them. This was the worst we had ever had and only by the grace of God and men like Paddy and Newsome, would we have escaped as we did. They knew just what to do, there was no panic but there was movement and it was quick.

Relaxing as we reached our particular bay, someone said to me:

"You are bleeding, Cooky."

I took off my cap and sure enough there was a wound in my head, then I noticed blood running down my arm and on to my hand. I had been hit in the elbow too. Yet I was the bottom man in that corner with seven or eight men above me or so I thought. The blast and concussion was terrific and everyone knew that, yet I was the only one wounded, so I was sent off to the Regimental dressing station further back in the wood. Reaching there, I reported to the Medical Officer who dressed my wounds. They were not serious so I thought and although he muttered something to the Corporal attendant, I went out and back to the trench.

This all happened so quickly that I found Syd looking very despondent and greeting me with"Where have you been? I've been looking for you all over." He had not heard about it but he had another worry. Whilst we had vacated our bay, we had left some rations in a little cavity in the parapet and they were gone. Yet that parapet was intact, How come?

Before work came tea, believe it or not, and seeing young Buttery opening a new tin Syd exclaimed "Hey, that's mine." Buttery told us how he found it where we had left it and as we couldn't take it with us, then surely he wouldn't have been daft enough to leave it to be blown away. Now it was his but he would share it and so the meal went happily on.

Soon I was told to report to Captain Prideaux our Company Commander. Entering his dugout, a mere shelter, he said:

"Ah Cook, I got a message that you had gone to Field Ambulance then heard that you were back here. Why didn't you go?"

I told him that I had not heard anything about Field Ambulance and did not consider that I was badly wounded. He told me I should have gone and could do so even now. He thought it would be best if I did.

"But Sir," I said "That might mean I would have to leave my friends and maybe come back to another platoon or even company. I would prefer to stay." He gave this some thought and then told me I could stay but need not do any particular duties and if the shelling started again I was free to leave without asking permission. This touched me as so far I had had little to do with Officers apart from taking orders and then mostly through an NCO. Captain Prideaux showed me the man he was with a real care for his men. I was to serve him for a long time yet and in a way he would never know.

It is fair to say that many of our Officers were as raw as we were, as General Sandilands says in the Regimental History of this time. There were few of the regular Officers left, Prideaux being one of them. The toll of casualties had been heavy in the early days of the war and still was. It was said that the life expectancy of a 2nd Lieutenant in France in the trenches was six weeks and I can believe it.

Strange to say I was the only casualty in the days we spent there. CSM Drayson, Sgt. Newsome and Paddy showed me every consideration and saw that I had everything Captain Prideaux had ordered.

The following night we were to be relieved by a Scottish Regiment but as we were preparing to leave we got a bombardment again and this was heavier than ever. Shells fell thick and fast and it was realised this could only be the prelude to a raid. Drayson and our NCOs had every man prepared, posted with rifles loaded and bayonets fixed with instructions that no-one opened fire until ordered.

"We'll see the whites of their eyes first" Drayson said "then let them have it."

Captain Prideaux was seeking a man to guide the relief in and Drayson suggested me,

"He knows his way about Sir, and can see in the dark. Just the man Sir."

I felt flattered and with instructions I went my way to the dump. As I left I heard the order FIRE! Then came rifle fire such as was never heard in Sanctuary Wood. Fifteen rounds a minute, it lit up the wood and gave speed to my legs.

Reaching the dump I contacted the company to relieve us to be asked by their Officer:

"What is going on up there?"

"When I left Sir, Jerry was coming over but he won't get far, our lads won't let him."

I was the butt of many Scottish swear words as I led them along, was accused of not knowing my way as they stumbled along like raw recruits, but I never made a mistake and reached my objective to find smiling faces and all quiet again.

"You missed it Wilf" Syd said "you should have been here it was terrific to glance over the parapet and see them hanging on the wire."

No one was interested, nor I, the sooner we left Sanctuary Wood the better for all.

Daybreak saw a mass of weary men trying to march but more resembling a football crowd leaving Elland Road, weary, mud stained, simply staggering along. A man here and there would fall with sheer exhaustion. To make any attempt to lift him up was to be told by an Officer, "Leave him, he'll come to and follow on in his own time", which they did. Hours later they arrived in camp in ones and twos, a pitiable sight but one that we had to become used to, particularly in the Ypres salient, the 'cockpit' of Flanders.

CHAPTER SIX
"IN DE PATRYS"

A few days rest was badly needed after our gruelling spell in Sanctuary Wood and this time we were to get it at Locre. This was a pleasant little village, although within range of the larger field guns and there were signs of a war being waged a few miles away. Tents were provided and we resumed the discipline of an established camp. The cleaning of uniform and equipment was possible but button cleaning was out, as a bright button or cap badge betrayed ones presence in the line. As the stiff wire in our caps had long been discarded, future issues were softer but steel helmets had not been thought of. Gas masks had been changed for a 'PH', a grey flannel bag with a mica eyepiece and rubber tube to breathe through. Placed over the head with the lower part tucked tightly into the tunic, one was supposed to be immune from poison gas but the weak spot was the mica which was liable to crack especially when being put into the carrying bag. Slung round the shoulder, it was with us all the time, even here, well behind the lines. It was soon found that the bag could also be useful for carrying small extras and it was said that a visiting General was caught during a gas 'alert' producing a pair of socks instead of the vital 'PH'. A snap inspection in our platoon produced some queer things, just as the breathing tube produced some rude noises known as 'raspberries'.

"In de Patrys" was a very good hostelry, standing on a little knoll overlooking the village and countryside. It was the venue for the old men of the village, veterans of previous wars, who sat for hours outside conversing with one another and no doubt passing their opinions of 'Les Anglais'. Few spoke any English but we exchanged a friendly greeting 'Bon Jour Monsieur'. Our French was slowly improving and we spent our off duty time pleasantly, sitting round a table eating 'pomme de terre fritz' and trying to talk to the waitress. At one café there was a charming girl but her English was nil. We tried to order two eggs each (it must have been near pay-day) but Mademoiselle didn't seem to understand. One of our number pointed to each of us in turn with the words "Deux oef", "deux oef" until at last she cried "Ah oui monsieur, je comprend. Chacun deux" and two well cooked eggs plus chips arrived on each plate. On subsequent evenings we all agreed we would go to "Chacun Deux's" place. She was a very sweet girl as I remember her. I never saw anyone in my platoon try to take advantage of any girl or woman, rather they were treated with respect. If we had any surplus jam or bully beef it was a welcome gift to these poor peasants eking out a living in dangerous surroundings. The younger men and husbands were serving in the Forces, if not already dead beneath a cross stating "Mort pour la Patrie." They lay in thousands already.

Our food whilst on these rests was prepared in field kitchens but we never got anything really appetising. There seemed to be no imagination amongst the cooks. It was stew every day. Breakfast would provide bacon but it was usually overcooked and by the time we got it was cold and with a layer of yellow fat. Occasionally the Orderly Officer for the day would come round to see if there were any complaints but I can't recall anyone making one. Had he done so, I don't suppose it would have done any good. There was always the excuse 'we are in the army now', and it seemed at times we were the lowest form of humanity as far as luxuries went. Our cooks were not popular and their treatment of the orderly men rather arrogant but their day was to come, as I shall relate later.

We made our own amusement and had many good laughs amongst ourselves. It was at Locre there occurred an event never to be forgotten. Pay parade took place and rumours were that English stout was to be had in Poperinghe. Once the parade was over there was a great deal of cleaning of boots and puttees and a general smartening up as a number of men set off for 'Pop' with five francs each to investigate the rumour. Sid and I did not join them. Yes, there was stout in Poperinghe, we knew that when the lads returned after a good night out but morning told a different tale.

That stout had never seen England or Dublin. It must have been laced with diluted Number Nines (a universal remedy for anything from earache to diarrhoea). The latrines were on the outskirts of the camp, very primitive affairs with a long pole suspended over a deep trench. This day the queue stretched round the camp as the stout did its deadly work. The sanitation men were kept busy and our considerate NCOs, several of whom were victims themselves, varied the training programme for the day with musketry lessons, as first one and then another flew across the field to join the queue.

Only once again I was to see the folly that could follow pay parade. Pay was handed out just prior to our departure for the line but with an hour to allow us to visit an estaminet or do some shopping. The result was disastrous and could have been much worse but for sheer luck. The lads went for the strong stuff to lace the penny blob, the maxim being 'today we live –tomorrow we die, so make the most of today'. Our Officers having managed to gather up the inebriated men, we finally took to the road to the strains of 'Blaydon Races'. The route was again towards the Ypres Salient passing 'en route' the famous crossroads known to us as 'Café Belge' after the hostelry of that name. This place had earned a reputation as a dangerous spot, enemy artillery being likely to drop a fusillade of shells any time day or night. It was no place to linger.

For some reason a halt was called right on the corner, simultaneously with another battalion on the other side of the road. It was a very dark night and as usual someone called out to see who the other lot were, with the reply "Northumberland Fusiliers."

"What battalion are ye?" someone cried, "We're the forst."
Equally strong Geordie voices replied

"We are the ninth, is our Geordie there?" and immediately there was pandemonium. The effects of the hastily consumed drink had not yet worn off and discipline was forgotten.

The 9th Battalion was a famous one, formed in Newcastle for the duration only and one of the 'Pals Battalions' part of Kitchener's Army. Here brothers sought and met brothers, cousins met cousins and others met an old 'marrer' from Byker or Jarrow. Heedless of the danger at the crossroads the jubilation went on, units becoming entirely mixed up in a huge melee. Officers and NCO's cried, "First Battalion men this side of the road" others "Ninth Battalion men come to this side."

Had any transport tried to pass it would have been carnage. Syd and I just stood and wondered how they would be sorted out again, if at all. Finally after much pushing and shouting some sort of order was restored and we moved off to loud cries of "So long Geordie hinny, we'll be seeing you on the quayside" or "divent forget to write home and tell them ye've seen me lad", and into the darkness we went. It had been a great occasion, so much so that the Regimental magazine made reference to it at home.

"Wherever ye gan you're sure to find a Geordie" is a Tyneside song and its truth was exemplified that night but not by one Geordie but hundreds. Payday had lent spirit to the celebration, short as it was. Although the Regiment raised fifty-two battalions in the war (more than any other regiment) it would have to be the ninth on a night like this. It was the topic of conversation for days. Who knows? Perhaps the Germans were celebrating a similar event that night for it was a miracle that we could stay there so long and not one shell fell among us. Had it done so the results would have been devastating.

Not all of us were Geordies but we were a happy band together, their joys were our joys and we stood together wherever we went. This time it was to a new part of the salient, for we were to be in reserve at Zillebeke, X Company being alongside the lake. Here were the remnants of houses, shell shattered, but still offering some shelter above ground and reasonably dry. To us this was a cushy billet after our previous dugouts, which were little more than a shelter in a parados. We heard of the enemy's deep shelters but so far none had been provided for us.

The weather was still fine and because we had to keep concealed as far as possible there was less work to do by day. We relaxed and listened to the tales of Sundays on the quayside at Newcastle or some other reminiscence but we were always on the alert for the occasional whizz-bang that came our way.

The Field Artillery was concealed all around us and their lives were no better than ours in the line were. There was also time to write letters home and receive mail. The field postcards have messages already printed just requiring the striking out of phrases not applicable such as "I am well", "I am in hospital", "Received your letters" and so on, just to reassure the folk at home. All other letters were censored by our Officers, except a green envelope, which bore a signed declaration that nothing within is of value to the enemy. Some men could not read or write and came to Syd or me to read to them or write for them. Many a family secret came our way and we conveyed many a kind thought to a sweetheart or Mother. I wrote several field postcards for one man and asked him how to sign them "Just put Woodbine," he said, "The old girl knows it's me and she never lets me down."

Sure enough within the week he came to tell me it had worked and I received five Woodbines for my labours.

Although censorship was strict I always managed to let them know at home roughly where I was by a code we had arranged before I left after my embarkation leave.

When I did get leave from France, the wall map revealed my movements perfectly. Father had followed me everywhere even to Zillebeke itself.

It was at Zillebeke where I had a preview of the kind of men these new friends could be in a real emergency. The platoon had settled down to what we hoped would be a quiet night having spent the day draining trenches in preparation for the coming winter. We had a comfortable little shelter and having blown out the candles we dropped off to sleep. It had become second nature to sleep whenever we could and no opportunity was lost.

"Stand to everyone" we heard the cry as guns opened up all round us, batteries we did not know existed were close by so out we tumbled.

"Fighting order and pick up two bombs quickly. Jerry has broken through Sanctuary Wood."

All sprung to it with bayonets fixed as we rallied round our Sergeant, then off we went in the direction of the woods. We passed men retreating who told us to turn round. "Fritz is on our heels," they said but we carried on following Captain Prideuax and ignored their fears.

Reaching the entry to the woods we paused and took cover in an old trench whilst our officers tried to assess the situation.

"Probably a small working party" Captain Prideaux said to the Sgt-Major. "They may have gone back with a prisoner by now. Send two men forward to reconnoitre"

Sgt-Major Drayson looked down at the men immediately below him and asked us to call out our names.

"Flanagan, Buttery, Jowett, Cook", we replied.

"Cook and Jowett Sir, both good men. They will go."

We felt proud to be chosen as we stepped up out of the trench. Our Captain gave us instructions "Go forward carefully about 200yds and then take cover. If the Germans should approach you open fire and we will come on and deal with them."

Off we went, following a rough track between the trees until we reached a place where a fallen tree offered just the cover we wanted. To our disappointment there was no sign of the enemy and we were eventually ordered back. This may sound dramatic but to us it was exciting with possibilities, which at a later date we would not have relished but we were still young!

Returning to our lakeside billets, Syd gave vent to his opinion of the men he was serving with. I still had some doubts whether he had really taken to the Tynesiders but now I knew.

"Wilf" he said "I have no desire to serve with any men but these. Could any other regiment find men who would turn out like that without a moment's hesitation when it looked as if all hell had been let loose."

He really meant it. I admitted it was remarkable. They were as enthusiastic as if they were spoiling for a fight. Then I remembered how we had run right under the muzzle of a gun, just as it fired. We could feel the heat of the flame but no one even ducked, we just raced on. (Later I learned that I had burst an eardrum). After the incident was over there were comments about men who panicked and turned tail. How it happened we never found out, probably some mistaken sentry seeing things in the darkness of the wood. We knew this regiment but it was not typical of the Midlands where they came from. We too had Midlanders in our ranks and they were all good soldiers.

CHAPTER SEVEN

TRENCH LIFE

The monotony of trench life as we led it could be relieved by a change of duty, especially where one could get away from the battalion for a spell with friends. It was just that little freedom from the strict discipline under which we all lived. Such a chance came to us as Syd and I, with four others plus a Corporal, were detailed for seven days guard on a vital bridge, known as Bridge 14, crossing the canal near Ypres, almost in the village of Kruisstraat. At night this carried much of the traffic to and from the Salient but in daylight it was under observation by the enemy, especially by means of observation balloons. The bridge had not to be used by any mounted men or any large parties and it was not a place to linger. In the close vicinity were batteries of guns, concealed, yet in action spasmodically day and night, which would draw fire from the enemy. We had to be alert and for our protection we were provided with the best dugout we had seen so far, probably built by our engineers, within easy reach of the bridge. The sentry stood on the banks of the canal, concealed by a sentry box dug into the embankment, not patrolling the bridge except at night under cover of darkness. It was not exactly a cushy number but I remember the comfort of something like regular time for sleep and the companionship of good friends. Our Corporal was an old hand and entered into our relaxation without in any way forgetting his duties. After trench life, this was a relief. Time passed pleasantly, although we heard the sound of guns nearby and saw the further disintegration of Ypres by the bombardment, which demolished the gasholder throwing debris far and wide. The bridge leading straight into the town, some half a mile away, was guarded by Military Police and seemed to be a particular target. At night we doubled sentries to cope with the extra duties of identifying traffic, which was heavy with supplies and regiments going forward or returning from the line.

A morning came when a Staff Officer and his orderly came mounted, to cross the bridge in full daylight.

"Sorry Sir" I said "You cannot cross this bridge by daylight and I must ask you to return the way you came. You may conceal your horses and go on foot providing you have a duty to do and we know who you are."

If looks could have killed, Private Cook would have dropped dead there and then.

"What do you mean, I've been over here before and I am going over again. Who gave you orders to stop me?"

"Those are my orders Sir, and you will not proceed further as I am going to obey my orders", this in a loud voice to enable my Corporal to be alerted in the nearby dugout. He soon appeared fully armed as I was with, bayonet fixed. Reporting what had happened he endorsed all I had said and told the Officer he was surprised that he did not already know that this route was forbidden. With visions of having to use sterner measures we glanced at each other for some moments, then his highness turned his mount and did as I had told him, proceeding on foot leaving his orderly to conceal the horse. His bodyguard told me what might happen to me for obstructing a Staff Officer. He evidently held him in higher regard than my Corporal and I did. We told him what we thought of Staff Officers in general and that as the 'Fighting Fifth' we didn't shirk our duty anywhere so they could 'get on with it!'

His Highness returned, still giving me dirty looks, to which I paid no regard, except to 'present arms' as he left, having been told by the Corporal that he was a Major and entitled to it but I begrudged it. Such men were few and the army would lose nothing of value without them but they took good care of their jobs no doubt.

Of different ilk was another Colonel who came to cross daily. On being told the rules he made no demur and complied cautiously. For several days he crossed and never without a courteous word, even asking my name and greeting me with a "Good Morning Cook." He asked me if I liked this post and I told him I would like it for the duration, he smiled and said "No doubt." How many Officers failed to show this little warmth, even as he enquired about our dugout and comfort?

The battalion passed across the bridge at night en route for Sanctuary Wood. Sgt. Newsome stepped aside towards me and said:

"Cooky, sew these on before I see you again" and disappeared into the night, handing me some chevrons. This posed a problem, still having no desire for promotion, here I was with orders to become at least a Lance Corporal though fortunately no one had seen or heard. The chevrons were passed to Syd with the Sergeant's compliments and he made his first step up promotion's ladder and one felt he would make a good leader having all the qualities of an Officer and a gentleman. I never regretted this. I did not consider that I was old enough to lead men some of whom were old enough to be my father. My ambition was to equal them in work and duties, whatever they may be. Syd had the extra pressure at home and I could see it was pleasing to him just to write and tell his family he had been promoted.

I had already learned the respect shown in our battalion to old soldiers; especially good regular trained men. Parades had been held where all Officers and NCOs fell out and the old hands appointed their leader. He took charge marching us all back to camp in perfect order, just as he would some day in action.

The politicians at home, the Generals and their Staff saw the war as a whole moving Corps, Divisions, Navies and Battalions at will, according to their judgement and the action of the enemy. We knew little apart from the fact we were here as volunteers to protect our country and our people from what we thought was taking away our freedom and way of life. No one took the trouble to tell us, although we read the newspapers as they arrived, usually late, and watched the action from what at times seemed a worm's eye view, knowing that without us the higher command could do nothing. There were times when we considered we were just cannon fodder, as the casualties mounted and our conditions remained the same. In retrospect it appears that much could have been done to ease our job and to improve our comfort. Not that we looked for luxuries but there was a gulf between the lives of the men at the front and those far behind the lines. It was ironic, as Captain Bruce Bairnsfather showed in his famous cartoons, that a sense of humour enabled us to keep going. One showing a man opening a tin of jam had the caption, 'When the hell is it going to be strawberry?' told the truth that we got what was left, not only of jam but other things. Plum and apple for us, with the occasional apricot, but those who handled the rations got strawberry and marmalade. Pay too was a grouse. The infantry man on a shilling a day and that reduced to sixpence as in my case when I made an allocation of the other sixpence to my Mother. Our Officers fared a little better but the Army Service Corps drivers and Ordnance Corps, who may never hear a shot fired, were on six shillings a day and so on. Imagine the feelings of our ex-miners when they heard of men at home striking for higher wages in an industry vital to our work. The shortage of ammunition and shells felt by us was in some measure due to the slackness of those to whom the war was a long way off. It is the soldier's privilege to grouse and he does but it is also a maxim that he does the job first and grouses afterwards and we did just that.

It is said in the regimental history that at this time, 1915, the battalion felt the loss of trained officers who had become casualties in the early battles. We were fortunate in having a few remaining who could train the newcomers to commissioned rank. One such was our Colonel, when I joined the first battalion, Colonel Yatman. Unfortunately, I was not to serve under him for long but his reputation was still alive and he was spoken of with pride by all.

After the battle of Bullewarde Farm at Hooge, on 14th June, it was said he was bringing back some remnants of men, about sixty in all, through Ypres. A sentry challenged him "What mob is this?"

"This is no mob, it is still the Fighting Fifth" he replied.

Others like him will follow in this narrative.

Our immediate officers we knew by sight and name but they seldom spoke to men in the ranks, except through the NCOs or we to them apart from answering a question. We respected them for their rank and looked to them for leadership as required. If one did fraternise just a little, he was the more respected and would receive our fuller co-operation when the time came. Yet I had some admiration for the young man who took on the responsibility of an Officer. There were times when he would have to lead us on a journey perhaps to some fatigue or a carrying party. It was his responsibility to lead us in the right direction, often by a map reference. Very few of us could read a map, as we had never had any instruction, so we found our way by instinct and experience. To enquire one's way in the Salient might bring an answer:

"You know where there is a dead man's hand sticking out of a parapet?" or:

"You will see a dead mule, turn right and keep your head down and straight on mate" and on we would go to arrive at our destination.

Our young Officer did not have to enquire, he led, and we followed. Often it would be through a shelled area, where our inclination was to take cover, but on he went, apparently oblivious to shellfire.

"Why the hell doesn't he wait until it quietens down" someone said.

Probably he would have liked to but it is infra-dig and strange to say it paid off more often than not. He was on his own as he led us, a man apart yet one of us.

Our days at Bridge 14 came to an end as we handed over to another unit and rejoined our friends in Sanctuary Wood again and heard what had happened in our absence. The woods were still a collection of trees; shells having cut down a few more but the snipers still worked from the treetops.

On the 7th October, Captain Gunner, our Adjutant was killed. He and Major Cruddas had been sitting in a sunny spot a considerable distance to the rear of the front line, regarding themselves quite safe except for the occasional shell.

Suddenly a stray bullet was heard to pass very close at hand and they considered it advisable to move to a safer part of the wood near by. They had barely risen to carry this out when Gunner caught his breath and fell. Major Cruddas thought he had just slipped but looking back, he was quite still and turning him over he found he had been shot in the head. Thus died a gallant Officer, a descendant of one who had fallen leading the 2nd Battalion in the storming of Badajoz, one hundred years before. The Gunner family had a long association with the Regiment. He had seven brothers who all served and gave their lives in the service.

Night patrols from our lines searched no-man's land regularly and brought in two prisoners one night. Interrogation Officers failed to get any information from these two scared men who could not speak any English, until one of our NCOs with a reputation for being a wise guy on language was brought in to help. With a mixture of Hindustani and pigeon French, each sentence ended with the reply "No compris", proving of little avail. The two Germans were sent back to Army HQ with the hope that sterner measures might reveal some valuable information. We had enough knowledge that Fritz sat in trees waiting to take a pot shot at us and an occasional rifle grenade told us they were still just 'over the road'.

We had the additional excitement of one of our machine gunners hitting a German plane which had the audacity to fly low, just skimming the tree tops along the length of our bit of line. He did it once too often.

It was said that one of our new officers had been heard to remark that when his servant had cleared his dinner dishes, he was seen to clean his knife and fork by sticking them into his puttees! These same servants were useful to us, bringing us all kinds of rumours gleaned as they served at table.

"The Kaiser is chucking his hand in favour of Little Willie", or

"Leave is starting again and it is to be for 14 days per man", down to:

"The Germans have a new kind of shell called the diarrhoea shell. It affects anyone near its explosion, making them dive for the nearest latrine, which is laid under the sights of a whizz-bang battery just waiting for the moment to come."

No one who was there can ever forget Sanctuary Wood, where one lived moment by moment and any rumour no matter how ridiculous, relieved the tension under which men lived. Little groups of men would be making a dixie of tea, sharing rations and cracking jokes at someone's expense. There I got to know men for what they were worth and names crowd into my mind.

Flanagan, Ginger Garland, Pozzy Gibson and Butterley with his everlasting song 'My Baby Rose, oh my little baby Rose', together with our Sergeant, Paddy the Corporal. A happy band of brothers! It was good to have this time and place to get to know them, for the future was unknown and could only be conjectured. It was supposed to be rather quiet here just now, at least our casualties did not amount to anything serious. Someone got a 'Blighty', a wound, which would just manage to get him home with the prospect of being there until the war ended. 'Lucky man' and we the unlucky cheered him off with "send us a postcard" or "don't forget the Woodbines." Mud caked us from head to foot; lice had taken possession of all our clothing worse than ever, as we had little opportunity for de-lousing but if one knew the ropes one could survive with a modicum of humour.

A battalion of another regiment from England came to have instruction for a few days from us, this being their first time in the line with even myself now being considered an old hand. They looked new with clean tunics and boots against our soiled ones. One man came to me one morning to say he had just seen a man with his jacket off and it was full of lice. He curled his nose up and said:

"Mucky beggar. How can anyone put up with that?"

I asked him if he had any lice on him and he was quite hurt at the suggestion. He was further surprised when I turned up the collar of my tunic and showed him my collection of 'chats' and their eggs, to say nothing of what I could have showed him if I had disrobed. Poor lad, he was quite shocked.

I marvel that we did not have an epidemic but few went sick and as I saw it, never without good reason. Our Medical Officer had a nose for a malingerer and a passion for giving out Number Nines, a pill which was the cure for everything from dysentery to toothache and an iodine brush which painted foot blisters and gum boils!

Someone came along with a tale that he was sleeping in his dugout and a shell came and took the sandbags off the top and left the corrugated iron.

"Just like that!" he said "and I never got a scratch, Bloody marvellous"

We all agreed. All sorts of things happened in Sanctuary Wood.

Men chose for themselves, at times, the fatigues they particularly liked. None were easy but men had different tastes, abilities and skills.

Natty Bell, a native of Armley, Leeds, was a bright and happy youth. He was just the man for Sanctuary Wood. His pet fatigue at night was the sanitary squad, which emptied the buckets from the latrines into a convenient shell hole in no-man's land and covered it with earth. At 'Stand to' we gathered round our Sergeant to discuss the night's work. Matty was the first to volunteer for this dubious honour. Syd and I preferred sandbagging or carrying rations if sentry duty was to be thinned out, as it often was. Matty did his job well, even being at his duty when the enemy probed the area with rifle fire. To our amusement, Matty cried out loudly.

"Will you stop that firing while I empty this s..t!" then calmly finished his chores.

It was a stray bullet, which finally lost our happy friend. Again, about his duties, a ricochet struck a tree and then Matty's arm, shattering it very badly from the shoulder. Matty took it all in his stride

"A Blighty one lads" he said "while I was emptying the s..t."

He was laughing as he left us. We never saw him again. Good old Matty!

All the men were tired, longing for the relief, if only for a few days but this was trench warfare. We accepted the daily casualties as a matter of course, the constant alerts, the 'process of attrition' which some believed would bring an end to the war.

Several spells with intermittent rest periods at camps in Locre, Reninghurst and that area, made up our service here. These camps were often a base from which we emerged at night to take supplies to those in the lines.

We manhandled loads of gas cylinders, barbed wire and duckboards and it could be really hard work. There were times when I was so exhausted and wet through that hearing a bullet whine close by or strike a tree, I wished it had gone clean through my heart. By morning we were back in camp, where all was forgotten for a while, as we ate the inevitable stew.

Eventually we moved further back to a village called Godewaersvelde and later Winnezeele and spent a month in rest billets. These were in barns on farms. Though not exactly luxury, it was very welcome and we revelled in it. The farm buildings were on three sides of a square, with a huge manure heap in the centre. Officers would be billeted in the farmhouse and able to live in a reasonably good mess. We had all meals cooked for us but still stew, stew, stew and to add to the mixture of vegetables, we had chestnuts.

These were horrible to me, turning purple when cooked and very indigestible. At least we could vary our diet by visits to the village and the 'pomme de terre fritz' again. The evenings at the estaminet provided us with comradeship, helped by the 'penny blob' of Belgian beer. We made our own fun, seeing nothing of the concert parties and entertainment, which the Y.M.C.A. were providing for the troops.

Our excellent Sergeant Major Drayson had his birthday about this time and was to entertain his NCOs in the sergeant's mess. The menu was centred round a whole pig, which he had bought from the farmer. This was cleaned and prepared by the cooks and hung for all to see on a tree near the field kitchen. All ranks went out to view this delicacy as one might view the hams at the Yorkshire show.

Late at night Jackie, Hughie and Co came home from their evening outing at the local and entered the barn where we were preparing for bed in the straw.

"Whee'se is the pig?" Jackie asked.

He was told of the birthday party that was to be held tomorrow night and his fertile brain got working. At daybreak the farm cocks crowed the reveille.

"Howay lads, breakfasts ready, come and get it" Jackie called and we rose to the sweet smell of bacon, chops, liver and everything a pig can provide. Nothing was left as we cleared the lot, with good wishes to 'Cock' and his family. The company cooks, on arriving to prepare breakfast, were not needed and much to their surprise...no pig, not a bone to be seen. This brought out the Sergeant Major himself with enquiries. He showed no sign of anger but he had a lot to say as he interrogated us.

"I know where that pig went lads and I know who took it. Look where I look."

He turned his gaze on Jackie and Hughie, standing all innocent looking and expressing sympathy to Cock for his loss but with no idea who the culprit might be. A suggestion was made that it could be the 'Jocks' from the neighbouring camps.

"Never mind lads. No hard feelings, I hope you all had a good breakfast" and Cock walked off to make other arrangements for his party, which in spite of everything, was a huge success, although we rankers were not there.

Only Drayson could do this and bear no malice. He liked Jackie and Hughie as much as we did. He had a capacity for giving and taking a joke. He could forget his rank, treat us as a man like himself and return to his status with no respect lost. None ever said a wrong word about him and Jackie and his pals would give their lives for him.

Of course the same providers were very useful in other directions. We noticed eggs were in good supply and occasionally chickens. One night Syd and I were returning from a visit to the village along a dark road. Hearing voices and a scuffling we noticed someone coming over a wall and were hailed with:

"Here, catch hod" and down came a chicken whilst Jackie and Hughie followed. One wonders what the Belgian farmers thought of us at times but no doubt they made allowances. Every one of them would have done military service at some time and their armies fared even worse than we did for meals. Soup seemed to be the mainstay and what I saw of it was very watery. However we left good supplies of bully beef, tins of biscuits and there was a very British Army look about the boots worn by both sexes around the farm.

Training still went on and we spent hours on drill, manoeuvres and route marches, just to remind us of the more serious side of warfare. Orders came that we were to move and we had to parade in full pack, nothing to be left in the billets, we were moving to an unknown destination. Having done fifteen or twenty miles we arrived back to find tea ready, the quartermasters stores and such establishments having had a quiet day. This led to much guessing and lessening of loads.

One such parade where it was said emphatically that we were moving, even the field kitchens were packed up and the Orderly Room paraded. Sergeant Major Drayson carefully inspected all ranks, even to feeling the weight of packs, haversacks, and water bottles, to see that nothing had been left behind. Taking his place like a ramrod in front of our ranks, it was noticed that straw was protruding from his pack. Someone offered to carry it for him but he only smiled, knowing that we had tumbled to a game any of us would have joined in had we known. A battalion of exhausted men returned to well-swept billets all too familiar to them once again. The freshest man after an exceptionally hard march on Flanders roads was Sergeant Major Drayson but we bore him no ill will.

CHAPTER EIGHT

OUR DAYS OF PHILANDERING ARE OVER

The pleasant fields around Voormezeele were disappearing in the distance. We really were bound for an unknown destination with all ranks fully equipped; Officers mounted and transport in the rear along with smoking field kitchens. Rumour had been rife. Officer's servants had supplied us with information 'straight from the horses mouth'! Some said Armentieres, where there were pianos in the front line and football was played in no-man's land or Hill 60, which was now standing on sticks, having been undermined by our sappers. Another strong rumour was that it was Mesopotamia or Egypt and the old hands had visions of wearing toupees again.

Finally we arrived at midnight in the middle of a large field, verdant, green and absolutely empty.

"This is your billet for the night" we were told "Make yourselves as comfortable as you can."

So we fell out without a blanket or a bivouac, only what we had carried with us. Now we saw the wisdom of retaining a long overcoat which some had cut down to a shorter length to lessen the weight of mud whilst we were in the trenches. It was a cold night as we wrapped our puttees around our feet for bed socks and lay on our waterproof sheets and gazed at the stars. Thankfully the British soldier can sleep anywhere and loses no opportunity to do so. No one got influenza with plenty of good fresh air and we woke refreshed and were on our way.

It was noted that the whole of the 3rd Division to which we belonged was on the move. We gathered this as we saw divisional signs on vehicles from various units. These signs were in general use now, whereas when I first joined one could read every Unit, Division and Brigade in plain English. The powers above us were very slow to realise that enemy eyes can read English too. We found we were to relieve the 24th Division somewhere near St Eloi and Verbrandenmolen, so all hopes of the sunny Mediterranean were gone and we were back on what might almost be called home ground. Winter was approaching and the rain had already increased.

At Dickebusch we were in billets again but only for a very short spell. Whilst our Officers and NCOs reconnoitred the trenches, decisions were made as to who went where. The Regimental Histories said there was little to report during the next three months or so. Diaries from both Brigade and Division reported as 'uneventful and quiet' or 'no incident'. So it might be to those who spent 7 or 8 days in the trenches then retired to a safer distance not so close to the watchful enemy, where they listed the progress of the war by moving little flags on a map. My own diary was a scanty one as it was not considered advisable to keep movements recorded in case one was taken prisoner.

About this time, some organisation at home had sent us a consignment of woollen comforts and I gained a nice pair of socks dyed navy blue. I had also gained a large blister on the sole of my foot during the last stage of our long march. Blisters usually received home treatment with a needle and a dab of iodine but this was just a bit too big so I reported sick. The MO did not apply anything more than I could have done myself and ordered me back to work. This was a carrying party to the trenches at St Eloi now knee deep in liquid mud. The return journey was agony as my foot pained me more and more.

Next morning I couldn't get my boot on and reported sick again. 'Field Ambulance' this time and I had to wait in Dickebusch for transport to Poperinghe, this being the night transport, which had been delivering, rations.

This turned out to be a vehicle drawn by two horses with two wheels and no springs, a sturdy affair but no ambulance. Together with a man with a broken foot, we travelled together in the rear of the box. Whether it travelled by road or over open country mattered little as we covered the distance between Dickebusch and Pop by the shortest route. Our driver mounted on a horse, ran across ditches, shell holes and tree stumps at an incredible speed. His passenger's groans and complaints met with no response, sufficient that we were leaving the Verey Lights behind.

Reaching 'Pop', we were left to make the final stages of our journey through the streets of the town to the Field Ambulance, two sorry figures limping badly. Feelings were not improved, as we seemed to be a joke to two women, who openly laughed at our plight. They certainly had no sympathy for us.

The doctor diagnosed my case as septic poisoning and I was given the comfort of an army stretcher on the floor for a bed. The treatment was hot poultices applied regularly for the next twenty-four hours, with an occasional inspection by the doctor. He seemed to be waiting for some major eruption but he eventually decided the moment for action had come and made an incision releasing the pus. The relief was immediate but I was to go to hospital as a stretcher case.

The hospital train was a haven of comfort. I was bathed and divested of dirty clothes and adherent lice and had a real nurse to attend to my wants. It was heaven and the destination was apparently Rouen.

Thirteen is supposed to be an unlucky number but I am not superstitious and for me it was a lucky one. I remember considering this as the train moved to its base among the many hospitals in Rouen. I joined up on the 13th of March, embarked on the 13th and was wounded on the 13th of September. The sign at the entrance to the hospital was plain enough '13th General Hospital' and as I was carried into a hut I noticed the door was labelled Ward 13. This was a new world to me but one fear came into my mind. I had left my friends and this might lead to my transfer to some other battalion or even regiment. I could not imagine anything worse and I was already wishing myself back with the lads.

Again I was lucky in my stay here, for the staff were excellent and spared nothing for our comfort. Sister Martin (God bless her) was the idol of us all. Not only was she good looking but also she was devoted to her work and was kind to everyone, regardless of age, rank or regiment. We were here to be made well and she would see to that. Whether it was that I was a mere boy to her or not, I like to think that she paid me a little extra attention and referred to me as her 'Little Fusilier.' She told me to forget about going back to the trenches for some time yet as my foot was in a very bad condition and would take some time to heal. How right she was. The poulticing began again but this time by gentler hands, finally being lanced from the heel to the toe.

My immediate neighbour was a man named Gregory, much older than I was and suffering from trench foot. This was a common complaint and most of the patients in the ward had feet protruding from the bedclothes, to allow their frozen limbs to thaw gently. Their toes were swollen and sometimes black. A nurse told Gregory that if she was allowed she could nip his toes off quite easily and he wouldn't know it. His condition got worse and the pain must have been excruciating, as I know he slept little. Sister Martin visited him often in the night and I, pretending to be asleep would hear her trying to comfort him. He was most patient himself but eventually the morning came when Gregory's bed was empty. He had died in the night.

My nineteenth birthday on December 5th was spent in this hospital. People at home would know that at least I had a clean bed to sleep on and a few cards and presents came. My father always sent me a large packet of Greys Cigarettes, which he considered the best, although he was no smoker.

Mother's gift was a home baked ham and bacon pie, which I always asked for.

Weeks passed as I reconciled myself to this treatment. All the men were friendly but I made no particular friend as they were from all parts of the country and few could move about. There were some sixty beds arranged on two sides of a large hut, scrupulously clean, well lit and warm with excellent food.

One night we were awakened by the lights being turned on and at the entrance to the ward we saw a little group of people, a Staff Officer of high rank in the Medical Corps, Matron in her red cape, several clerks and our Sister Martin in the rear. They began their ward round, looking at the medical charts, whispering a few words at each bed, until they came to me.

"And how is the foot going on?" asked the Officer.

"Very well Sir, I think it won't be long before I can get back to duty again."

The Medical chart went back on its peg and there was no comment but a strange look from Sister, which in my innocence I did not understand. When the party left there was a hubbub in the ward whilst everyone inspected his chart. There was jubilation in the air and it still hadn't dawned on me why, until Sister came quickly to my bed.

"Fusilier, why ever did you say you were getting better? Everyone in the ward is going to England but you." she said and turning to the others:

"Some of you are lead swingers almost. Fusilier here has done more real soldiering than any of you and he'll be weeks before he is fit for duty. There was nothing I could say. I wasn't asked but I could have wept when I saw he had been passed by and you lot are going home."

I could see she meant it and later explained to her my fear of being sent to another regiment. I must have been a mere child to her, but I overcame my disappointment. Christmas came and went and I was discharged.

There was a strong belief and not without cause, that we infantrymen, known already as the PBI (poor bloody infantry) were looked on as some sort of inferior being, whose only place was in the front line and any time out of it was a waste of man power. Hence once out of hospital, back off leave or having a few days at the base for redocumentation, the sooner he was back to the land of blood and sweat, the better. The infantry base at Rouen was one of several I was to experience before my soldiering days were over. This was a huge camp well removed from Rouen itself which was 'out of bounds' except to the privileged few and those who were fortunate enough to get a special pass for a few hours within this famous city. It was not my good fortune although I never made any serious attempt to go.

I was content to hear the stories of its nightlife and the occasional fracas between the PBI and their arch enemies the Military Police. Along with the staff of this god-forsaken camp, their object in life seemed to be to get rid of us as soon as possible. They were universally disliked because of their overbearing manner, loud mouth and no guts. Cleanliness in the camp was a matter of strict discipline and there wasn't even a tab end amongst those tents. The dining hut smelt of carbolic soap as did the utensils, and the food had little to commend it, being principally bully beef and stew *ad lib*.

The Bull Ring was a large area of ground for exercises and drill, all to be carried out with the utmost vigour, although it was like 'teaching a grandmother to suck eggs.' We could handle rifles and bayonets far better than most of the instructors but they wouldn't admit it.

One of our own Sergeants happened to be there at the same time having also been in hospital. I knew him well as he served in my company and liked to give the impression that he was a friend of Sgt. Major Drayson, which I doubted. Although a regular soldier, he was not very tall but made up for his lack of stature by his conduct, which earned him no friends. The only thing I will grant him is that he was no coward in danger but a martinet in other ways. Here he was given the job of instructing in bayonet fighting at which he fancied himself.

The equipment was an advance on what we had used before, consisting of reinforced leather jacket and helmet, with wire mask and various protection such as used by fencers. The rifle was fitted with a blunt spring bayonet, which was very heavy. 'Buck' our diminutive Sergeant who had earned the nom-de-plume in the company, took it upon himself to don the armour and show us how things should be done. He picked the man for his opponent, a big fellow but obviously a man of the soil, lacking in agility and a bit heavy on his feet. So David faced Goliath, each prepared to give the equipment a good testing, Goliath being told to attack as if he meant it. The children of Israel, ourselves, awaited events.

The attack opened by a strong lunge to David's midriff, a swing of the butt as his feet were taken from under him and he got a terrific clout on the jaw, followed by a butt in the ribs as he lay prone.

"Lay off you b....y fool are you trying to kill me?" he cried as he rose looking even more diminutive than ever.

Goliath said no more for he had just done what he had been told to do and those who remembered the Sergeant's reputation congratulated him and were only sorry that it had ended so soon. This would be a good story when I got back to the lads, one Buck would never tell against himself.

There was no regard here for comfort. The Medical Inspection entailed standing unclothed outside a hut in a long queue, frozen stiff. A quick check and we were pronounced 'Fit- A.1.' and despatched, being the next consignment of cannon fodder, as far as the staff at Rouen was concerned. So once again I took the train back to my real friends.

CHAPTER NINE

THIGH BOOTS, GENERALS AND MUD

January-February 1916. The winter was well advanced when I rejoined my company still in the region of Ypres. During my absence they had a long period of rest in back areas but had spent Christmas Day in the trenches, 'with suitable fare' says the History. I can imagine it! I was told little of any celebration so it cannot have been anything very special. No fancy hats but there had been pudding well frozen from a tin.

As if they had been waiting for me, they were not long in moving off to the line again and this time on a bitter cold night, with snow and drizzle, bound for what was known as the 'Blood Tub', sounds inviting! After some hours on the march we reached a communication trench and were told to change into rubber thigh boots. These were provided on the spot, probably left by some unit who had used them before. In the darkness and confusion I was unable to find a pair to fit me at all. Time waits for no man here so I was told to come along into the trench and a pair would be found for me in the morning. I dropped up to my thighs into the coldest mud I ever knew and we waded on regardless, to reach the front line and relieve those who wasted no time in clearing off.

"Good luck chum, it's cushy here." they said, "we haven't had one casualty. Fritz is just as wet as we are and he isn't interested."

We found this to be very true. Dugouts were nil, lots of snow and Company HQ was a lean-to contraption in front of the parapet, actually in no-mans land, where our Captain kept his lonely vigil, no better off than we were. To move about was to wade through the liquid and the only comfort was to sit with knees to chin on a firestep made of broken duckboards. Sleep was impossible so it became a doze with a rifle between the knees. The first time I did this I was awakened by a splash as my rifle had fallen out of my grasp and I fished it out from the bottom of the trench.

Sergeant-Major Drayson brought me a pair of gumboots, which I put on over my already soaked trousers only to find that they leaked. To make tea we had not a single piece of dry wood but a good supply of candles, plenty of water but not for drinking as someone had lost the tins on the way up. Melted snow is a poor substitute, especially over a candle flame, but we still made tea of a sort and chewed on frozen biscuit and bully beef. Even the humourists among us could not rise to such an occasion as this.

Our then Regimental Quartermaster, known as 'Cush', was a teeto-taller and sent us pea soup powder in lieu of rum. We vowed never to sign a pledge again and used the powder to dust our socks later. It was true that the Germans fared no better. We could see them baling out just as we did, but with little effect so we waved to them. At daybreak one morning two German Officers were seen strolling in no-mans land as if it was a park, gesticulating as they talked. They could have gone further, for what we cared but our Officer thought it inadvisable and we sent a few rounds across but not meaning to hit the target, so they took to their lines unharmed. We were told that we had six days here before we would be relieved.

Amongst our visitors was Brigadier Potter of the King's Liverpool Regiment. Along with his staff and our Adjutant Captain Pease he entered our bay and indicated we were not to move from our perches on the firestep. Before he rounded the bay to leave, one of our lads called him back:

"Hey General, when are we going to be relieved?"

Instead of being shot for insubordination, the General turned round and said:

"I'm sorry for you boys. I'm doing my best to get a relief but it is three days march away yet. I'll have them here as soon as I can, meanwhile stick it out and I'll see you'll have a good rest when they come." He moved on but not before our Adjutant told our spokesman:

"That was not the way to address a Brigadier." We all thought it was good for a laugh.

Soon it was evident that trench foot was affecting everyone. Every night at sick parade first one and then another failed to return. The Captain told me himself that if everyone who had trench foot went sick he would be left alone and he was suffering too. He allowed thirteen men a night to go and we tossed for it. My lucky number again but I decided not to take part in the gamble. I would see it through if it killed me.

After six days the relief came but we were only to move to the second line reserve trenches. Had we known they were dry and unoccupied we would have been there already. The trenches in the second line had good shelters, a shattered building and it was possible to light a fire with wood and coal which someone had kindly left there. The only drawback was the number of dead men left lying about from some recent engagement of the Welsh Fusiliers. Why they had not been buried or removed I never found out and as far as I knew no one made any attempt to do so.

We were too busy filling our frozen guts with hot tea. A petrol tin with the top cut off did duty as a kettle and was refilled as fast as it was emptied. There were lashings of tea; sandbags full saved from the last six days and sugar in abundance with Ideal Milk too. Never did men drink so much tea before and never did men sleep as soundly as we did. The General kept his word and orders were given that we had to get all the rest we could but we never undressed as we were too close to the line. After a few days we moved at night, with the promise that if we reached Vlamertinghe, a train would be waiting to take us back to Poperinghe.

Our journey was along the disused railway track. My feet were like hot cinders, every stone a knife as I plodded along, supported by someone in less agony with the words:

"Stick it out Cooky, don't miss the train lad. It's a hell of a way to Pop."

At last we reached the train of covered vans in total darkness and I was hoisted up like a sack of coal and immediately fell asleep. By daylight another man and I awoke to find ourselves at Pop station, the rest having marched off without us, knowing we could come in our own time. Still we could not make much progress and decided to sleep on the pavement so we dropped our equipment and lay down from sheer exhaustion. The townsfolk were asleep too.

"Messieurs, vous burez du café" I heard someone say as I was shaken awake. Heaven has no angel to equal this lady of Poperinghe who took us in and gave us cups of steaming coffee with sympathetic references to "Les pauvres soldats, vous etes beaucoup froid." Refreshed to some extent we left her with many "Merci beaucoups" to find our friends in the company. Enquiries soon led us to their billet, a disused factory building. They had been there for hours and had finished breakfast. Immediately eager hands were ready to help us. Sergeant Newsome took me in hand and tried to remove my gumboots. He had to cut them off, as my feet were red raw and very painful. With rest, food and dry clothes I was able to go with the bath parade in the afternoon. This was supervised by the RAMC with tubs of steaming water and showers and we were soon engaged in removing a fortnight's muck.

Whilst I was dressing and trying to get my socks on the RAMC Corporal came to tell me I had trench foot and advised me to see the MO I told him I had just come from hospital and did not want to go back yet. I would stick it out. He strongly advised me against this but seeing I was adamant, gave me instructions how to massage my feet with whale oil, which fortunately was in plentiful supply. This would restore the circulation. I persevered with this treatment and without missing a duty, regained the use of my feet. Days later postcards began arriving from some who had gone sick and were now in England. Once again I had missed the boat.

I asked myself these many years later, how it was that we never heard of Toc H. whilst we were in Poperinghe. We made our own amusements between duties and drills and could rarely afford to visit the YMCA and Expeditionary Force canteens. Syd and I were both practising Christians and would have been delighted to go there but we were never told about it when we needed it most. Was it because we were in the PBI!

The war had now entered a New Year 1916 and we were still stuck at Ypres, with an occasional advance of a few yards of trench at great cost, only to give it back with more loss of life. Rumours abounded that we were going to be the spearhead of something big. Our next move was to be around St Eloi and we rehearsed over fields laid out with white tapes to show the route we would take in the dark. We kept this secret and could only guess what the target was to be until we were told that we were to take the Mound of Death itself. We knew it had been under-mined having taken loads of explosives to the engineers there at night and emptied the spoil for them.

We were further encouraged by being told that we will be supported by the biggest concentration of artillery ever to be assembled on any front. Some 500 guns plus a 12 inch naval gun, which we were warned had a very low trajectory, were set to fire over our heads on to the enemy's front line. Furthermore we were to be equipped with steel helmets for the first time. We had often envied the Germans their inverted chamber pots and were now to be equally protected. We were to be supported by the 12th West Yorkshire Regiment, our close and valued friends in the Brigade. The Royal Fusiliers, also friends of ours, were in it too on the left but the main objective was ours.

So this is it, my first time 'over the top' and I listened to advice from the old campaigners. A further surprise, we were to be transported by London buses as near as possible to the scene, during the night. The same buses would wait for our return next day. We did not expect they would need as many on the return journey, but it sounded good.

As this narrative is not a history and dates are more or less insignif-icant, I will return to incidents prior to St Eloi, which remain in my memory.

CHAPTER TEN

THREE MEMORABLE INCIDENTS

Private Henshaw was a very good soldier, who hailed from Stafford-shire. One only had to hear him speak to recognise that. He was a very likeable fellow, quiet and unassuming. He was a stranger to the Geordies as were others from different parts of the country. We had Londoners too amongst the regulars and also a few Irish.

During one trip into Sanctuary Wood we had a particularly rough time, when sleep was at a premium because of continuous shelling. Henshaw was doing sentry duty alone in a bay. He felt extremely tired and fell asleep standing up at his post. On one occasion I remember nearly doing the same and resorting to chewing tobacco to keep awake, spitting the brown fluid at the Germans. Henshaw didn't know this trick and never heard the visiting Officer with the Sergeant (not Newsome) when they came along. Speaking to him he never replied and they brought Flanagan as a further witness to his lapse of duty.

He was later tried for his offence and sent for Field General Court-Martial. Things looked serious as he could be shot at dawn as things stood. Flanagan gave evidence at the first trials and confirmed what had happened. To us he said very little, although we questioned him. None of us wished to see Henshaw punished for what we could all have done in similar circumstances.

At the final trial at the General's Court with all the trappings of Military Law, things looked black. The first witness was Private Flanagan:

"Did you Private Flanagan on the night of.... See Private Henshaw asleep at his post?" The reply came without delay but caused a stir.

"Yes Sir I did, just as I should have been had I been on duty there." He was asked what he meant.

"Sir, we had all been without sleep for three days and nights and it is the rule by King's Regulations that sentries be posted double in the front line at any time, certainly in such circumstances as this was."

Flanagan was a serving soldier, he knew the rules and had never told us what he would say and wisely kept it until the highest court met. Had he said it before it would have been quashed. The Officer in question was questioned and reprimanded for neglect of duty. The court stood down and the verdict was to be given at a later date and read to all ranks by the Commanding Officer at a full parade.

This day arrived and we assembled, fearing for our pal. The Colonel read out the charge and the sentence of the Court, which was 'Field Punishment for Life'.... Bad enough but better than 'shot at dawn'.

This means that Henshaw was to be a prisoner when we were at rest but to take part in all work and duties in and out of the line, also he received no pay. He rejoined us prior to our next trip into the Salient and we talked to him in the billet. He was very depressed and talked of his wife and family, saying he hoped to be killed on this trip. Sergeant McClochlen said to him:

"Don't say that Henshaw, it's cowardly to wish yourself a dead man. Keep on hoping. 'Life' means the duration of the war and it will end some day."

Henshaw was not appeased and we all wanted to help so much that we gave him special care and tried to cheer him.

Our particular destination was a position known as Zouave Wood, an isolated trench behind a crater at Hooge, used as a reserve line covering open ground. Entry was by night only and no one could leave in daylight as the enemy knew we were there and we were a special target. Fortunately he never dropped a direct hit but always near enough to cover us with flying steel. Henshaw was beside me when a shell fell within feet of us and he got a huge splinter in his head. He cried out in his Staffordshire drawl:

"Give me a handkerchief somebody, I'm bleeding to death" someone gave him a large red handkerchief and I saw him put it into the hole in his head. He collapsed and died quickly by my side.

I've seen many men die, as we all had, but never did I see men so affected as they were over the death of poor old Henshaw and what was said to the Sergeant who was one of his accusers, would not bear repeating. He was glad to be transferred.

One of the favourite magazines of the day was 'John Bull' edited by Horatio Bottomley, who was a well known journalist and very outspoken, especially about the war and the conditions for the troops. He published an article, 'Shot at Dawn' in which he exposed the wrongs of Court Martials where the prisoner had a poor defence if any, and the sentence had no appeal, nor was the victim told of his sentence until a few hours before its execution.

This caused a furore and things were altered and made more humane. In fact it was to be abolished altogether. How many men suffered death like this before the article appeared? There were other punishments in the field, which were a disgrace to humanity, but little is said of them. I once saw a man at Reninghurst fastened to a gun wheel, that punishment went too in time.

Zouave Wood was our home for six days and our only other casualty was Captain Fielding who had wounds to the face, being caught in the open near his dugout. He was the only Officer with us and was well respected. On one occasion when we had managed to make some tea, I took it on myself to offer him some, as he had no servant with him. I shall always remember his gratitude and his asking how the men were faring and what they felt. I put the best face on things, hoping to ease his anxiety.

Close to the end of the trench there was an empty machine gun emplacement with a good roof of corrugated iron and sandbags. It was just the place for a quiet kip if we could get there. Six of us decided to risk it at night. A quick dash between the shells for a few yards and all could be well. We poised, timing the fall of shells and finally made the dash. As the next shell came, we were all scrambling to get through the door. It hit the sandbags on top sweeping them far and wide. Now everyone wanted to get out and the race went to the strongest. Once back in the trench unharmed we all laughed and accused one another of being 'windy' but it was a near thing we often joked about.

Hooge is a name stamped on the memory of every man who ever served in the Ypres Salient. Never a day passed by when Hooge did not get its share of hate. Men would watch from a distance a black cloud of bursting shells and hear the roar and say:

"There can't be a man left in those trenches in Hooge", but there were men left. We learned to hang on, past masters in the art of avoiding shellfire, although we often sat in the bottom of a funk hole or under a bit of corrugated iron, gritting our teeth and holding our jaws in case someone heard our teeth rattling! When it quietened down, the stretcher-bearers came along and another one started his journey to England or else to one of the nearby cemeteries to join thousands of his brothers. Here was the famous crater left by a land mine exploded under the enemy lines in July 1915 and men still lay there awaiting burial, some still locked in attitudes of combat, some said. It was a grim sight and I only once ventured a quick glance into the depths. It was no place to linger; Jerry was only a stone's throw away.

After 'Stand to' on this particular morning, there was a heavy mist and our acting Sgt-Major McLaughlin thought we should clear the old jam and bully tins carelessly thrown over the parapet rather than buried. They were food for the swarms of bluebottles and the rats, which plagued us. We suggested to him that this was a risky business so close to the enemy but he thought otherwise. He ordered Buttery and two others to go over. As they climbed over the parapet Buttery said:

"Someone is going to get killed on this job."

Hardly had he spoken when there was a volley of rifle fire, someone said:

"Roll him in" and he rolled in right beside me –dead. At the same moment the post Corporal came into the bay. "Buttery" he cried as he rounded the corner, "There's a letter from your Mother." Then he saw him lying there and tears came into his eyes.

This was a sad start to the day. We had lost our brightest character. Buttery was a young man from West Hartlepool who once went to Lister Street School as I did. He loved to sing as he went about with a smile on his face 'My baby Rose...' Whenever he could he referred to his mother and everyone in the platoon had seen her photograph at some time. He was so proud of her. She looked like him, a cheerful woman, hard-working and full of character. We hoped she would never know how he died. He gave his life doing his duty but at a task which should not have been allotted to anyone that morning.

This incident was followed by a bevy of snipers, for the mist was clearing slowly and we had other casualties further along the trench. Not to be outdone, we took up the challenge and every man became a sniper determined that Buttery should be avenged. There was no doubt that this was so, as the targets were plentiful, the Germans trying to take advantage of the remaining mist.

Captain Prideaux came along to join in and went into a saphead in front of the trench proper. He was observing over the top and we could see the back of his head. He wore his hair close cropped, similar to the Germans and his head was bare. "I'll get this one," said the man next to me. The Captain never knew I saved his life for my friend could not possibly have missed at 20 yards. It was an exciting morning but a very sad one and probably the saddest man of all was poor 'Paddy' McLaughlin, for he was a kindly man and well liked. He was a regular soldier and had been chosen to be in the Guard of Honour at a recent visit of HM King George to the armies in the field. I saw these men parade before they left us and they were a credit to the Regiment and were all over six feet tall.

The third incident happened in Sanctuary Wood again. 'Stand to' was over and we were settling down for the night duties when we got a terrific strafing on our particular part of the trench. It seemed to be aimed especially at us as if Jerry wanted to wipe out X Company. Shells fell in pairs mixed with whizz-bangs, 5.9's, howitzers-the lot, a really concerted effort.

There was no question of evacuating, as there was no time, so we retreated to the bottom of the trench as low as we could go and hoped for the best. The Sergeant thought, as we all did, that this was the prelude to a raid but no one wanted to stand and watch for them coming over in that holocaust. Luckily it blew over and luckily there were no casualties but how we escaped was a miracle.

"Who do you think is the bravest man in this platoon?" asked Sgt. Newsome as we were discussing the attack the following morning. We looked at him in surprise, as this was not a question we discussed. He repeated the question and obviously had something on his mind. We mentioned various names but he shook his head at each.

"I will have to tell you," he said. "We were lying in the bottom of that trench last night, scared stiff knowing that any minute Jerry could be over and in. 'Pozzy' stood looking over the top and saying to me down below "I can't see them yet Sergeant but I'm keeping a good lookout and if they do come I'll open fire and let you all know."

"He did this the whole of the time. How he didn't get blown to bits we will never know but for sheer bravery and coolness in the face of death I hand it to 'Pozzy'." We stood there and for myself, felt ashamed, as others must have done too. 'Pozzy' is jam in army slang. Gibson had a great liking for jam hence his nickname. He was a bit of a 'loner' with no particular pal and we just accepted him as one of the platoon. Now we saw a different 'Pozzy' and he earned our respect. He wouldn't lack jam from now on but a Military Medal would have been more appropriate had we had the power to give him one.

There is a sequel to this story, which I found out later when I was on leave.

My Father was an insurance agent in Leeds. His calls took him into the poorer parts of Hunslet. Calling at a house in Joseph Street where families lived in a cellar kitchen in back-to-back houses. He found the good lady sitting near her fire with a telegram on her knee and tears in her eyes.

"Trouble, Mrs Gibson?" he asked.

"Yes Mr Cook. I've just learned that I've lost my only son. He was all I had."

Father was a good Christian and just the man to give her the only comfort anyone could give. I knew there would be a prayer and sorrow shared. My Father said there had been little jam in that home at any time. Asking her what regiment he had been in he learned that he was in my platoon, which helped him to comfort her further.

Years later there was a memorial cross outside Christ Church in Meadow Lane with his name on it. I never passed the spot, now cleared for road improvements, without thinking of him and I salute his memory.

CHAPTER ELEVEN

OVER THE TOP

The camp at Reninghurst was where we made our final preparations for the great event before us at St Eloi. There was no stinting on equipment. If one needed a new pair of trousers or a tunic it was to hand at the stores. We cleaned and checked everything. Ammunition was cleaned round by round if one had any sense. Dirty cartridges can jam a rifle and no one wants that to happen. Field dressings and emergency rations were renewed and nothing was left to chance. Personal things were sorted out to see that nothing took up unnecessary space even in a pocket that was not wanted. One had to think that in the event of being a casualty, identification was needed and letters etc would be sent home. Not that Syd and I had anything to worry about there but he was loath to part with the many letters from his Lois.

I've never met Lois. I wish I had just to tell her how much he loved her. Sorting out the letters he would say:

"Wilf, I must keep this one, just listen to what she says..." and I would get some nice home news about people in Shipley, Bradford. Lois must have been a lovely person. Letters were written home warning them that we may not be writing for some time and not to worry. We went shopping for the little extras and I remember I bought a new pipe just in case the one I had got broken. My pipe was a great comfort in times of stress; for one thing it stopped my teeth chattering.

Our new steel helmets were not too popular as the fit was rotten. There was only one size as far as we could see and we had to cover each one with a sandbag for camouflage, otherwise they were almost heliographs. No one has altered them after all these years so they must have some appeal.

Our final armament on the person was two Mills grenades, primed, and everyone had one for each pocket. All were told the various jobs they had to do, this causing some overlapping of companies. I was posted to Y Company for the day in a bombers sandbag party.

We had to follow a bombing squad down enemy communication trenches and build barricades, which eventually I never did. Syd was on some other squad and being a Lance Corporal took the leadership.

The London buses materialised and we were off. Next stop Dickebusch. This was something new to many of us but far from the comfort of the London service. There were no windows in the bus, just boards and on the top deck instructions to 'mind the wires' and it was 'no smoking please'. The date of our departure was the evening of March 26th.

There is no need to go into the plan of attack, sufficient to say that we fortunately had a quiet night for the assembly in to jumping off positions, all done in silence. I found myself lying behind the front line. It was dark with just slight drizzle of rain but strangely there was grass under foot.

At 4.15am we were to begin exploding some 40 tons of ammonal in six mines under the mound of Jerry's trenches. Then the guns would open up and after two minutes we would be off (the two minutes were to allow the debris to fall). Someone had slipped up already, as two minutes is a long time, especially in the suspense of moments like this.

I was dozing with my face to the ground and my head on my arms. There was not a sound except the far distant rumble of someone else's battle. Suddenly a shrapnel shell came from our lines and burst over the German line, just one but it was like bonfire night at home, it looked so bright, then all hell let loose. This was the alarm –4.15. Dead on! The earth beneath me rocked like a ship at sea. One could see the movement and up went a huge tower of fire, earth, sandbags, duckboards, bodies and the whole was now indeed a Mound of Death.

No two minutes could keep us pinned down. We were up and off as we had been drilled, first to get over the old front line where little bridges had been set but there seemed to be only one near my squad and everyone made for it. We scrambled over as a machine gun opened up. Fortunately his aim was bad and we got through. In the glare of mines still burning in the sky and the flashes of gunfire exceeding anything we had seen before, men were racing on. Reaching the German line we found we were late in the race and looking down we could see the trench was packed with men under a sea of tin hats. Ginger and I slid down to join them. As they spread out there wasn't a German to be seen, until we spotted a party of them running away from us and we opened fire. Ginger and Flanagan made a beeline for a dugout and were souvenir hunting. It was not their first time 'over the top' and they knew the value of souvenirs in hard cash. It seemed most important to them to have first pick. What happened to the bombing squad I was supposed to be with I never knew but there was no lack of jobs for us. Everyone else was on his toes and opened up with rifle fire to add to the pounding the next line of German trenches were getting.

As daylight broke there was a lull in the activity near us so we took stock. Sgt-Major McLaughlin came along to say he had just left Captain Carrick and his bombers further along and they were having casualties and needed help. Asking for volunteers brought no immediate response so he asked if anyone could throw a live bomb. I told him I could, so he asked me if I would go and thinking that one place was as good as another, I said yes. Then he asked if anyone had any water in his bottle as he had used all his. Someone produced a water bottle containing cold tea. Paddy lifted it to his lips and said:

"There's rum in this" and handing it back to its owner said he would get a drink elsewhere. We knew that he was a staunch teetotaller and although the rum was very little he refused it. He moved away round the bay and almost immediately a man came round with the words:

"Paddy McLaughlin is dead."

"He can't be. He's only just left us," we said.

It was true. In those few seconds he had left us to walk right into a sniper's sights and was shot through the head.

I wasted no time in going along to Captain Carrick, there to see him alone and his bombers all lying dead at his feet at an intersection of the trenches. Telling him who I was and who had sent me, he asked if I had any bombs. I brought out the two from my pockets and he told me these were all we had.

"Will your rifle work?" he asked.

"Yes." He told me that there was a German with a rifle who kept poking it round a corner and he had caused most casualties.

"Get him if you can" he said so taking up position I waited but soon saw a white rag being waved at the end of a stick from a very close position.

"They want to surrender Sir" I said, "shall I call them in?"

"No don't trust them, it may be a trick and there are only the two of us."

I pointed out it was worth the risk and he told me it was on my head if I wished.

"Come in" I yelled and waved my arm as they came round the trench. There were thirty-five of them, still with grenades hanging from their belts but obviously scared. Some were wounded very badly, obviously from the Mills bombs thrown by the men dead at my feet. Carrick told me they had run short of bombs and had thrown German bombs back before they exploded. As the prisoners came in, I had my hands full disarming them. One, an Officer, said: "Officier." I told him that made no difference to me and to move along with the others. Taking his revolver from his holster I handed it to someone who had appeared from somewhere. Later I recognised him as Captain Hodgkinson. I never got the revolver back which annoyed me next day as they were bringing a good price from non-combatant troops, Canadians in particular.

I asked Captain Carrick if I could take these prisoners back, to which he agreed. Indicating that they should get out of the trench they filed out and made their way to our old line over the open ground with me trailing. We immediately came under machine gun fire from the German line, which lent speed to us all, until we reached a breach in the old parapet. The last man stuck in the narrow space and bullets were spattering at my feet whilst I shouted at him to get in.

To prompt him I poked him in the rear end with my bayonet. He shot through like a cork out of a bottle and I lost no time in following.

Seeing them as far as battalion HQ where I handed them over I retraced my steps. Reaching the branch and preparing to go across to rejoin my company I was stopped by a West Yorks Officer who pointed out a line of dead lying where I had just recently crossed.

"Those were my men" he said "They went out to dig a communication trench but a machine gun got them all."

I told him I must rejoin my company, come what may. I was not going to be charged with desertion but he insisted that I stay where I was and that if there was a counter attack, I could go but it made sense to stay here for the time being. Finally he told me it was an order so I had no alternative but to obey him and I joined the other men in reserve.

This must have been well on into the day as the shelling had increased as the German artillery had come into action and mortars came over in clouds. To add to our fears were the low trajectory shells we had been told about. They seemed almost to cut one's hair and sounded like an express train. They must have been deadly where they dropped. The German fire was mainly on this trench, presumably they knew reserves were there and all we could do was to try to find a better hole if there was one. A man with me suggested moving into the next bay but I told him to stay put. One place was as good as another here but he insisted and moved to the next bay only to return immediately with a hand missing. He had walked right into it.

In situations like this one only sees what is within vision. It was apparent that we had taken all our objectives and were holding on. Wounded men coming down told us that it was hell out there but everyone was in good spirits and there would be no giving way at all.

I was still worried about returning but I could see that to cross under this fire was impossible so I resigned myself. We found a little shelter to sit in and soon lost all sense of time. Eventually we noticed feet passing in file past the entrance and men's voices:

"Who are you?" I shouted.

"The Canadians" came the reply.

"Come on lads, that's enough for us. We were told the Canadians were to relieve us and that once we saw a Canadian we had to clear out without waiting for any orders."

This was quite true and we acted on it knowing that if we could reach Dickebusch the buses would be there waiting. So ended the day for me, in rags, covered in mud but still unharmed. I took my seat on the bus and wondered what had become of the others. Where were Ginger, Syd and the others of our platoon? Poor old Paddy McLaughlin wouldn't come back. I remembered how he had kept his temperance pledge to the very last and thought of Buttery who had been a victim of a sniper too. The two names will be in my memory forever.

Years later I visited Ypres with my son and his wife. We stood reading the names on the Menin Gate and Laurence spotted a name he had heard me mention. *Sergeant-Major McLaughlin, Northumberland Fusiliers*, one of the thousands with 'no known grave'. I wondered what happened to his body but I had seen what shellfire can do, there is little left for recognition.

Back at Reninghurst men were coming in all the next day in two's and three's. The regimental historian says:

'The appearance of the Fusiliers when they came out would have surprised their friends, perhaps shocked them. They had no apparent reason for cheerfulness but merry they were though plainly tired out. They were disguised in mud from their boots to the crown of their steel helmets. Their faces were swathed in ragged scarves and the ironmongery on their heads covered with canvas. They carried German helmets on their rifles and shuffled along to absurd songs. They looked more like the veterans of Agincourt come to life again and glad of it, than any likeness their home folk could call to mind. Their eyes though red-rimmed were impudent and gay.

It was so that those who had fallen would have had them return from battle'.

Casualties were officially:

Officers – 2 killed 4 wounded
Other ranks- 29 killed 125 wounded 21 missing
Prisoners captured – 5 Officers 195 Other ranks.

The Royal Fusiliers who had taken another flank in the attack were less fortunate, they lost 264 all ranks.

The battalion had another honour in that English papers at home gave a full account of the battle next day and this was the first time that a battalion had been specifically named. Newcastle must have hummed that day. No one wanted to sleep until he had heard other stories of the day and the search for pals or news of them were vital.

The historian confirmed my belief that the two minutes wait was a mistake as the falling debris did us no harm and we lost only two men on the way over. One of these may have been the fellow we heard shouting from the depths of the crater that he had evidently fallen in. As we flew past we heard him shouting above the din.

"Gan on the Fifth, gan on me canny lads" he was probably a football supporter!

Another story went on the rounds and was confirmed. When crossing the trench we came under machine gun fire. 2nd Lieutenant Holmes and Lance Corporal Kiersley were mentioned as having put this gun out of action. They went behind it and killed five machine gunners with bombs and bayonets.

Syd and I were glad to meet again. He was unscathed and had been in the thick of it. He told me that though the squad never got to do the actual job they were supposed to do, they found plenty of action.

Captain Pease, our Adjutant, came into the hut we were occupying seeking me. He asked me where I had been and whether I had been with Captain Carrick. I told him what had happened. Captain Carrick had been recommended for the Military Cross for that action. He was frequently mentioned in despatches and later earned a bar to his Military Cross.

As battles go, the action at St Eloi was a small affair and what it achieved was not going to end the war. Ground gained was lost later but we removed the mound, which had been a source of trouble for a long time and cost many a life. When I visited St Eloi after the war the craters were duck ponds with live ducks swimming on them. On a later visit I found they had been filled in and ploughed over.

The historian makes no mention of the succeeding night. We were turned out of our beds and told to gather together round the water cart to be addressed by a General. He told us we had done well and praised us all but he said the Royal Fusiliers had met with stiffer resistance and had failed to take all their objectives. If the position was to be held it was vital that these were taken too. The Royals were in no state to undertake the task and he wanted us to go immediately and finish what they had failed to do. We knew the ground he said, as he had no other unit who could do it and once it was done we were to have a long rest.

The audience passed remarks I dare not repeat. I was standing at his feet and heard it all. Opinions of Generals were aired and it was suggested he should go himself. The Adjutant told one individual that it was a General he was speaking to. The reply was that it made no difference, let the ... go himself and take his brass hats with him.

However we did get into fighting order, collect our bombs etc and left for Dickebusch but it came to nothing as a despatch rider overtook us with orders to return.

It was said that the Chaplain Captain Noel Mellish, hearing of this, had told the powers that be that the men were in no fit state to do the job. He had seen at first hand what we had done and his word saved us from what could have been disastrous. The Divisional bombers made an attack with blackened faces and were repulsed, the Canadians held on for a while and even they had to relinquish much that we had won.

Captain Mellish was awarded the VC for his work bringing in wounded under fire. He was new to us and we later learned to love him for the Christian he was and his courage at all times. Too little has been recorded of this gallant man and I will try to fill in some gaps. No mention was ever made of his servant who accompanied him wearing the khaki of the Church Army but not a member of HM Forces, an unknown hero.

Awards made for this action were:

DSO to Colonel Wild.

Military Crosses to Lieut. Carrick, Hogshaw, Holmes, Jones and to Captain White (Lieut. Carrick was later promoted to Captain).

DCM to CSM Cooper, Sergeant Carlin, Lance Corporal Kiersey (the machine gun incident) and Pte. Trobe.

At a later date there were added seven Military Medals, a new decoration for good service in action.

Just one little incident and the story is over. Sergeant-Major Drayson asked me to act as runner to a 2nd Lieut. saying:

"Cook will you look after this new young Officer we've got. He is very green and I think you will help him get on to his feet."

It was an appeal and a compliment I could not refuse and I remember him asking me several times how I was getting on. If he was green so was I.

My charge was feeling the cold and asked me to take a bottle from his dugout and make him some hot rum if I could. The only fire I could think of was in the Sergeant-Majors dugout, where by some means he had procured a coke fire in an old oil drum. Taking in a little old milk tin about half full of rum I asked Drayson if I could 'hot it up' on his fire. It was dark in the dugout but the coke fire gave a glow as 'Cock' and his friends sat round. I placed the tin delicately on the stove and waited for it to boil. It smelt good.

"It must be about ready now Cooky" Drayson said and I struck a match to see. It went up in flames immediately and Cock and his pals roared with laughter.

"Didn't you put any water in Cooky? Raw rum on a fire lad, what did you expect?"

I had to go and tell my Master that his hot toddy was 'kaput' It took me days to overcome the leg pulling and my friendly Sgt-Major thought it the funniest thing he had known in the trenches. However the officer was a gentleman and bore no ill will. In fact when he left the regiment he thanked me for helping him to settle in.

We left Reninghurst and St Eloi and had a longer rest in the village of Boeschepe and then Meteren. Here we celebrated St George's Day with the traditional red and white roses in our caps. This is the day on which the regiment honours their patron Saint all over the world wherever they are serving. A special church service is held, known as the drumhead service and we even trooped the colours as near as we could. It was certainly a good parade and everyone turned out spick and span.

I remember this day particularly as I was now a bandsman.

CHAPTER TWELVE

MUSIC! MUSIC! MUSIC!

Following the action at St Eloi the Orderly Room had extra work on their hands and they needed some clerical assistance. Syd was detailed to return to his pre-war profession for a while. Now we had another source of information with facts not rumours from Syd.

He came to my billet to tell me of a conversation he had heard during his new duties. The Sergeant of stretcher-bearers had been to report his casualties and to seek more men, preferably men who had been bandsmen. Syd knew I had been a bandsman at one time and told them of this so he was sent to order me to report to the bandmaster at once. I was not pleased, as to leave my pals and the company after all we had been through together, was unthinkable. I told Syd so but he advised me to look at it differently. He would be leaving soon in any case, as there was every indication that his application for a Commission had been agreed. Furthermore he said it was time I had a change and that the men at HQ Company, which included the band and stretcher-bearers lived just a little better than the men in the companies. Another thing he pointed out was that he had been ordered to send me there so I had to go to the interview at least.

Reluctantly I went, my feet dragging as I obeyed the order. It was a despondent man who found the bandmaster, a Corporal May. I was handed a trombone and told to play a few scales. In spite of not having touched an instrument for nearly two years I succeeded and he called for a man named Tommy to come and hear me. Tommy was a very big fellow with a cheery face and played the first trombone. Hearing my playing, which can't have been much good, he said:

"Good tone, Punter, he'll do. I'll take him in hand and bring him on." I learned that Punter was nickname of the bandmaster but how he got it I never discovered. Arguments were to no avail so I had to say 'goodbye' to my old pals, move to a new billet and get to know a new set of men.

These men were to play a great part in my future but first I must tell a little of how the band came into being.

The regiment had left their band instruments at home when embarking for France. It was considered that big drums and all the paraphernalia of a band were superfluous to requirements and bandsmen became stretcher-bearers to their respective regiments. They never had the right to hold the insignia of the Red Cross, only an armband with 'SB' on one arm. They carried no arms but the enemy was not likely to accept them as non-combatant, wearing the badge of an infantry regiment. They brought wounded from the scene of action to the battalion dressing station, where after attention by the Regimental Doctor, they became the responsibility of the RAMC. I think this appealed to me more than the musical part of the work.

The war had settled down to a static position in the trenches with occasional periods of rest. These men I had now joined had found some instruments in a deserted village bandstand and that formed the beginning. The Officers helped by having instruments sent out from home. Their first performance was in Dickebusch and other bands followed their lead. Of course the Scottish Regiment could not operate without pipe bands and many pipers earned VCs and other honours in leading men into action under fire. We had become attuned to the sound of the pipes from dawn to dusk, as we had in the brigade Gordons, Scots Fusiliers and others from time to time. A lone piper would be sent as a matter of course to lead a party to a fatigue when out of the line, even if the party was only a dozen. He would rouse men from their sleep in the morning and lull them to rest at night. Practising seemed to be at any time and one would see him in shirt and kilt (no tunic for this was in his leisure hour), pacing back wards and forwards playing away to his heart's content. What the tunes were we did not know but his comrades found it acceptable. Not so we 'Assents', especially during the afternoon siesta when we could get one.

It did not take me long to realise that I was the infant among men much older than I was. Their long service badges and Indian Frontier ribbons marked many years of army service.

'Punter' was not a Geordie but a southerner who had joined this northern regiment as a band boy, hence his knowledge of music theory. He played the clarinet, was a likeable fellow but a bit aloof from the others. He wore his stripes to give him authority but this was never taken very seriously by his men. 'Punter' he was and 'Punter' he remained, even to me. His ambition was to transfer to the Royal Marines when the war was over, then join the band and take a course at their excellent school of music. He had already been to Kneller Hall. He preferred playing his instrument to conducting and would lay down his baton at the slightest pretext and take over a solo part. When we were packing medical equipment and stretchers for transport to the trenches, every effort was made to see that Punter's clarinet was left behind. Once settled in some dugout, a few moments peace would be broken by the strains of Handel's Largo or scales in E Flat major.

"How the hell did he get that in the cart?" someone would ask. They preferred killing time by playing cards but I liked to listen to his delicate playing.

The most outstanding man was McQuade, 'Smiler' to all, even the Colonel himself. He wore the ribbon of the Military Medal awarded to him at St Eloi but he only wore it occasionally. When told on parade that he was improperly dressed without it he would fish it out of his pocket and pin it on beside the Indian Medal which he always wore. He was tall, very thin, turning grey but had a ready wit and his language was interspersed with Hindustani. He was an oboe player of no mean talent. The instrument was new to me, having been in a brass band, but I learned to appreciate it more than any other instrument in the band. If I had my time over again it would be my choice without question. It was noticeable that everyone looked up to him, with good reason, for this man had everything that makes a good soldier. He was cheerful, encouraging and as I was to learn later, fearless. We became friends in spite of the difference in our ages. I was always 'young Cooky' to him. He will figure in this narrative many times and will never be forgotten by his friends.

Tommy Nichols was the next outstanding man. He was a trombone player 'par excellence'. At our first rehearsal I listened spellbound as he played a solo from Gilbert and Sullivan's opera 'Patience'. I had never imagined a trombone could sound so sweet. He wanted to transfer to the euphonium and did all he could to help me take his place but I never reached anything like his standard. He never reproved me for the mistakes I made but he was far in advance of me and I felt rather discouraged. He was not everyone's favourite character. With his strongly built body and bearing, he could seem overpowering at times but beneath it he had the kindest disposition. He was a married man and a regular soldier with many years of service behind him.

'Dub' Sutherland had no equal. He too was an old regular soldier; he came from Sheffield although I do not think he had any relatives. He was a mystery man but a most likeable one. 'Old Dub' as he was known was an apt title, as he looked old to all of us and in his dry humorous way he played an old man with elegance. He was an excellent French horn player and seldom needed a score as he remembered every piece that had ever been in the repertoire of a military band. With his dry wit he could have us in tucks of laughter whilst he had a face as serious as a judge. He ate little, smoked fags to their stub ends and never complained no matter what we might be suffering in work, discomfort or danger. I think he and Smiler were the two most loved characters of the lot.

All these men had served together in the regiment in India and elsewhere and the army was their home. They came out to France in August 1914 and had seen all there was to see of action.

'Cosh' Hill was quite different. He belonged to Derby but spoke more like a Londoner. He played 2nd or 3rd clarinet. As he told me he was there to put the 'chuck chucks' in and never aspired to anything else but he was a useful member of the band and popular in his own way. He was easy to get on with, a generous and happy companion whether sober or drunk and it was in the latter state that he liked to be. He was not physically strong, probably due to the jungle fever he had suffered in India, but he never complained. 'Cosh' seemed to be able to put up with any kind of discomfort, whereas we would always try to make some sort of a bed, in barn or dugout 'Cosh' would just lie down and sleep like a baby.

Paddy Creighton was of course an Irishman of the kind one soon gets to like. He played the flute and piccolo and could also take his place on the side drum. Another regular, he had been brought up in the army from infancy and originally belonged to the Fife and Drums. (Regiments have these in addition to the full Military Band). Paddy was a man who would have made an excellent NCO in the ranks for he had all the qualities of a fine infantryman. He was fearless and another humorist like Smiler and Dub. Like Cosh he loved a drink and the stronger the better. Sometimes he could be awkward but never violent or quarrelsome. He was also a gambler and would stake his all on two match sticks floating down a stream so he was either in funds or skint but it didn't matter, he was still as cheerful as ever.

Amongst the others, some dozen or so, each had his own idiosyncrasies, the only one of note being George Fuller. He was a cockney and how he became to be a regular Fusilier I never knew but he had been in the regiment for many years. He had a cockney sense of humour and what's more he looked like a cockney! Small in stature, quick in his movements, a ready repartee and a great capacity for getting on the right side of people, particularly the providers of rations.

What better man to be our cook and it was in that capacity I remember him. George could make a meal fit for the gods anywhere and anytime and he was never happier than when he was dishing it out to us with his own hands. Along with Cosh he played 2nd Clarinet. I always used to think that the reed made him better looking beneath his little moustache and his merry eyes. The audience would recognise him as our cook by the smoke-stained uniform he wore. We still had no change of outer garments but George wore them with pride, even to shining his buttons, something we had long since ceased to do. Everyone loved George. He was our comfort in distress, not only good at providing food but also of many cigarettes when supplies were low. He was a prolific letter writer and would borrow a writing pad and sit in a corner happily writing for hours. When he brought back the depleted writing pad with very many thanks and a winning smile no one ever complained.

Following the despatch of the mail we waited and after a week or so the Post Corporal came round (I am remembering a time when we were out on rest). He was a great friend of George's, probably a 'townie', he would be made a special brew of tea, they would swap fags and then we would learn that a parcel had arrived. Near St George's Day the box was a crate and extra men were needed to deliver it to our billet.

"They are lovely girls you know, they always were, the girls of Newcastle are the best in the world," he would say.

So this is where the letters had been going, to the girls of Bainbridge's Clothing Factory in Newcastle, sort of 'friends of the regiment' and of course of George. The box contained everything a lonely soldier could hope for; cigarettes, tobacco, cakes, pies, canned fruit, socks, scarves, handkerchiefs, writing pads, envelopes and there was nothing those lovely girls had missed out. They must have loved George and he must have put a lot of time in with them when the regiment was in Newcastle. I said George had winning ways and any girl could not fail to fall for George. He had other providers but the girls of Bainbridge's were the best and if ever comforts were very low, we would ask George to write to his lovely girls and give them our love.

Sergeant Carlin DCM was our SB leader for discipline and our link with authority and the Medical Officer along with 'Mudgut', his RAMC orderly. The nickname was a reference to his portly figure and not used in his hearing. He was a very good medical orderly and along with our MO Captain Gill RAMC was never awarded the recognition which they deserved. Theirs was a silent service, a very grim one at times and took them, like us, into very great physical danger but they never flinched nor refused a call to save a man. Being RAMC he did not live actually in our mess, he and Sergeant Carlin dined with the MO in the dressing station.

As Syd had told me, life in HQ detachments was just that bit better than in the platoons and the SB's had just the edge on the Signallers and transport men, although they had their own Messes. The big advantage was that rations were given to us in bulk according to our number. Our cook, George, was able to select the best cuts of meat and bacon or anything else worth bringing back from the stores. Bread, butter and jam etc. was put into a large box from which we helped ourselves and no one took advantage of this.

The work of a stretcher-bearer was very worthwhile and gave more satisfaction to me than being a bandsman, hard as it could be. We had four teams of four men when at full strength.

No.1 team was made up of the strongest men-Sgt. Carlin, George Stoneham, Tommy Nichol and Punter.

No.2 team was the next fittest men.

No.3 were men with less stamina than the others but nevertheless did equally good work.

No.4 was known as the 'bone-yard', and was made up of Cosh, Dub, Gildy and others who were not known for their prowess in carrying weights at speed from difficult and dangerous places. Usually they were assigned to bringing out the dead, where speed mattered little. Perhaps this is unfair as they all did a good job and never flinched. At the call of a runner or signal from HQ we turned out immediately no matter what we were doing. To be told that we were wanted in 'B' trench or elsewhere and approaching to see it under heavy shell-fire was no joke but we went in, picked the man up and manhandled him back to safety as quickly as possible. I had very little medical training and the others not much more but the MO told us to forget the iodine etc. and get the casualty out just as he was.

We only bandaged the wound with a field dressing and the Sergeant carried a larger shell dressing. In retrospect, this was a poor way of treating men but whilst we did all we possibly could to ease a man's suffering higher powers decreed supplies and the 'PBI' did not warrant more. Casualties in this war must have been greatly increased by such cheese-paring of essential first-aid equipment. Not until a man reached Field Ambulance did he get any real comfort and many hours might elapse before that. If ours was an errand of mercy it was with empty hands through no fault of ours.

CHAPTER THIRTEEN

KEMMEL

After attending practices, which were always enjoyable, the band led the battalion away to pastures new. We left Meteren feeling better for the rest and marching was easier with a band to lead. This gave me an opportunity to get to know my new friends better, between playing and during the hourly rests by the wayside. There was speculation as to where we were going but we already knew it was in the direction of Ypres. Enquiries from neighbouring troops produced the disquieting news that the trenches we were to occupy are famous for trench mortars rather than artillery fire.

The battalion headquarters were in a farmhouse and we had a billet in a brick building in the farmyard alongside the dressing station. This was very promising and seemed to be made just for us. The farmer's family was still resident, as were some on neighbouring farms in spite of the frequent shellfire. The companies took up position in the trenches and we awaited their call. We had not long to wait. The signallers received a message that there were wounded and gave directions so off went No.1 stretcher. I followed with my party right up to the front line itself where my old friends of X Company greeted me. The man we came for was already dead, badly wounded by a mortar in the chest. I took hold of his head and someone else his feet to lift him on to the stretcher. His jaw drops and blood runs out of his mouth. It was too much for me and I had to say I could not do this, it almost made me sick. Taking my place they said: "Never mind this time lad. You'll get used to it. We all felt like that the first time. It takes time!"

I was able to help in carrying and learned how heavy a dead man could be, plus the fact that the trenches winding as they did, was not easy passage for a stretcher. We had to lift it above the parapet in places to get along, which gave Jerry a chance to take a pot shot at us and place another shell or mortar bomb where he knows there are a number of men.

Fortunately this time we got away with it but we had to carry the stretcher for almost a mile with little of that over open ground meaning that only two of us could operate at once. This particular spot had many memories for me and I visited it years later to see the graves of men we buried. Two were good 'mucking in pals' Shannon and Day. Day was about my age and from a good background. He had lost a hand when we got to him and looked as if he would survive to be treated successfully. He was quite conscious as we carried him down and handed him over to the MO but he died in the dressing station. This shook me again –one of my old and valued friends to die like that. I wondered if I had failed in doing all I could for him but it was to become known that very few men survived losing a limb. On enquiry, those missing arms and legs would have had them amputated under anaesthetic by a surgeon. The shock had a great deal to do with it, as the MO said time was essential and it was a job for him rather than some amateur playing about with tourniquets and iodine but we were still not quick enough. Shannon was also one of my old section and he was so badly wounded that we knew at once we should lose him before we got half way back. We buried them wrapped in blankets while Captain Mellish read the service, as we stood round with bare heads, a common sight in Kemmel. One such funeral was taking place as the enemy guns were searching the area with occasional shells. As the service was being read and Captain Mellish in white surplice stood his ground, the shells would fall quite near and shrapnel splatter about us but no one moved nor did the Padre hurry his words.

No Germans were going to prevent our friend being laid to rest in a proper manner.

Someone did confess later that he had a strong desire to jump into the grave as he kept his eye on the shell getting nearer and nearer. He was not the only one as their newest recruit felt the same.

Leading from the farm to the ridge where the front line was, there ran a light railway now in disuse. One bogey was intact and the lines too, 2 feet gauge and running up what was known as the VC road. The dead we left to bring down under cover of darkness, crossing over open ground and standing stock still when a Verey light lit up the countryside. Here Fritz had in addition to his star shells a searchlight, which played down on the VC road at times. We had the bright idea of using the bogey and railway for transporting two stretchers down at once and I joined in.

All went well on the way up but progress was slow as the wheels lacked grease and enemy ears were listening. The vehicle had not gone far from the line when the searchlight came on and had us in its beam. There was nothing we could do but stop and immediately 'freeze'. Any movement would have given us away and the machine gun would have opened up. Whether Jerry was suspicious or not we never knew but he kept us fully exposed for a long time. Not a word was spoken but gradually as in a very slow motion film four men shrivelled and tried to get under a very small bogey, their hearts in their mouths. The lights went out with a click and we took to our heels down the track, noise or no noise, sparks flying from the wheels until we were in the farmyard again. The others came out to see what the row was, imagining some new kind of weapon. All they saw was four scared men who once in safety laughed at themselves, each accusing the other of being scared. I accused no one for it was a near thing, which we never tried again.

I was to find, as in the days with the platoon, that there is a lighter side to war. Our farm was some distance from Locre where our HQ was. Mail reached us at night along with the rations, by horse transport, but the journey could be made in daylight by pedestrians willing to take just a little risk of a random shell. Permission was given for two men to go back to Locre to bring the mail and whilst there, might do a little shopping, a few fags or perhaps a bottle of wine would be welcome. This worked well for a few days and no one suffered for the two missing men. We could cope with all calls on our services.

The time came for Creighton and Dub to go for mail which usually took three hours. The day waned and still there was no sign of them. We were getting worried. Carlin sent us around the countryside to see if we could find them. As darkness fell without finding them, he was frantic. If they didn't turn up and the CO found out there would be trouble.

After breakfast next morning they turned up quite casually as if they had been nowhere. Carlin was furious:

"Where the hell have you been all this time? We've searched all night for you. It's the last time anyone goes for mail, you'll wait till night in future." The two culprits just listened quite at ease.

"Look Sergeant," Paddy said, "We were in no danger. In fact we were a lot safer than any of you were." And with that Carlin had to be content.

Later we learned what had happened. They had gone into an estaminet. Paddy got into a card game and drinks were so liberal that they could not complete the journey, being very tired. Seeing a very neat and freshly dug trench they made it their bed, a very sensible thing to do. When Paddy woke up to a bright sky.

"Be jabers" he said "I thought it was the resurrection mornin' and we were just over the road from here all the time."

This caused roars of laughter. Our pioneers had just dug that grave yesterday and it was only 100 yards away.

The war had become static. In France the two opposing sides faced each other across no-man's land with anything from a few yards to a quarter of a mile between them. The French were holding out but they were losing heavily at Verdun. Our routine was a few days and nights in the line, a few days rest in some back area or perhaps just in reserve with hopes of some leave whilst first one and then another came and went on their allotted five days. The Officers fared better with more regular leave at three monthly intervals but all leave could be stopped for an indefinite period. The system was by rota and one did not know how far down the list one could be. It was just wait and see.

Whenever we got a few days rest in Locre or elsewhere we took up our instruments again and practised either in the corner of some field or if we were lucky we might be in an estaminet or farm building lent to us by the owner. Sgt. Carlin, or more likely Fuller, who had a way of ingratiating himself with farmer's wives, would have arranged this.

His job as cook entailed his early rising to prepare breakfast, which was always ready for us on time. The quality never failed. Bacon and eggs cooked by George on an open fire were a feast for the gods. 'Madam' who had to get up even earlier to feed her husband and the chickens, as well as doing the milking, no doubt received tit-bits to add to their meagre diet from our Chef. We noted that on one farm where we had the very best of comforts, there was a coal fire, plenty of eggs and potatoes. We asked no questions when we saw Madam and George exchanging pleasantries at any time of the day. She looked old enough to be his mother or even grandmother but he said she was the best of all the Madams he had met in our farm billets so far.

At breakfast one morning we noticed that George was very quiet as he went about his tasks. Madam passed across the yard but looked the other way as we sat round the fire eating. We sensed something was wrong. Eventually George said:

"I had a bit of trouble this morning and it is worrying me. I just don't know how to get over it." He looked crest fallen.

"I was getting some potatoes from the store over there" he said "and the door opened It was Madam herself and she was as surprised as I was but not as uncomfortable. The worst of this is we've been such good friends. There was nothing she wouldn't do for us all. We never had anyone like her before."

"What did she say George?"

"That's the worst of it. If she had asked me what I was doing I might have explained or if she had gone off the deep end I could have taken it but she just turned away and left and you see how she passes us now. I'll be glad when we move from here lads." and poor George nearly wept.

When we did finally leave it was without one wave of the hand from our hosts, not a word but we did leave a very good cache of useful stuff which she would find later and perhaps she might forgive him.

This period around Kemmel was a happy time, not as happiness is measured at home but mixing freely with different units from other regiments around us. It was a great uplift from Sanctuary Wood and Hooge and the trenches were slightly better too. It took me some time to settle down to my new duties although I often visited my old pals where I was always welcome.

Syd had gone to his Officer's Training School but this bunch of splendid men I came to admire more and more than compensated for his absence.

In addition to those already mentioned, band practise helped me to get to know the others. The bass drum was in the hands of 'Darky' Matthews. He was once a clarinet player but had taken up the drum after the loss of some previous trained drummer and soon became quite proficient and evidently enjoyed his job. He was a great pal of

Cosh's but smarter in appearance, realising that the drummer was the centre of attraction and often the recipient of glasses of beer when we relaxed.

'Darky' was also a regular and as his name implied, had black hair crowned with a shiny bald patch and a neat black moustache. He had good looks and a happy smile and fitted in well.

Alongside him when playing stood George Stoneham with his side drum. George and Tommy were the smartest men on parade, always well turned out and one could imagine that in peacetime with the busby and full dress uniform they must have been an impressive sight.

Along with them had come another from the ranks, Harry Robinson, a Yorkshireman. He was an ex-miner from Rothwell, a father of a family and certainly at the extreme end of the age limit when he joined up for war service. He was a very good musician from a brass band, once a flugelhorn player, now given a baritone, which he played extremely well. Harry was much loved by these men who had never met a real native of Rothwell before, with his dialect and words which were familiar to me but needed explaining at times. He was quietly spoken, never in evidence but chipped in now and then with a dry humour of his own. When it came to drinking, Harry could see them all under the table and they admitted it. Being an old man to us, he was relegated to the 'bone yard' but proved himself a far better man than most.

Along with Smiler they made a fine pair, both being clay pipe smokers, black twist being their favourite weed when it could be obtained. He would sit in a 'pitman's crouch' smoking and enjoying a little black clay, his thoughts far away with his family in Rothwell. Sometimes he would chuckle as Smiler twitted him for his 'Tha knaws' and other expressions; Smiler being a southerner was equally a bit of a joke to Harry.

Band practice usually caused a few laughs or rows according to the mood of the men. Once Tommy took exception to Mick Creighton's piccolo part telling him he was out of pitch. This roused Mick to tell Tommy to play it himself and to our surprise he took the piccolo from Mick and signed to Punter to lead and he played the part as he thought it should be played. The ensuing argument brought the practice to an end and no one dared to laugh until we were well away but such disputes never lasted and there were no hard feelings.

Tommy's versatility got him into several disputes. He even criticised our conductor once and when Punter handed him the baton in desperation, Tommy mounted the box and proceeded to lead us. This was too much for Smiler and Co so we made a mess of it just to annoy him. This led to Tommy throwing the baton at Smiler and stalking off in high dudgeon, remarking that those with long service thought they knew it all.

'Dopper' Preach was another regular with long service in India who played our G trombone. The story was that he doubled with the string double bass and one night having indulged rather well on some patent brew, he returned to the barrack room and fell through this instrument. He was fined £200 to be debited from his pay. Now 'Dopper' had a streak of the Yorkshireman in him, coming from Sheffield, and he knew how to look after his money so this was the unkindest cut of all. 'Confined to barracks' or 'Pack drill' he could have done but to have to pay hard cash was too much. He decided to sign the pledge and from that day as long as I knew him he was a strict teetotaller. Poor Dopper, he later lost his eyesight in the course of his duties as stretcher bearer but I heard from him after the war. He was a versatile musician and we non-drinkers would spend an evening with him in some billet where he would go round and play every instrument, brass or reed did not matter but 'G' was his favourite. He was not a very tall man and always looked out of place on the march in the front rank with that extra long slide. We usually put him on the pavement side as we passed through some town or village and he loved to sweep the end of the slide at some Mademoiselle's feet as they stood watching us marching by. They could not see his face, for a steel helmet entirely obliterated him to his nose end. 'Dopper' and I were great friends.

Leaving Kemmel we moved a lot and training became more intensive in between short spells in the line and sundry fatigues for the battalion, such as taking supplies to units in action. We changed camps often, sometimes marching all day and were lucky to finish up in a village with some empty houses or a camp with tents.

On one occasion we arrived at a tented camp after a very long march, playing as we went. We dropped our kit and instruments and looked for a place to settle down. Dub came into the tent and put his French horn down near the foot of the pole. Someone shouted 'Blankets up' and dropped a roll of twenty army blankets through the door landing smack on the French horn.

A French horn is the most delicate and complicated of instruments. It was never made to support a roll of blankets and the result was a mass of flattened brass. Dub picked it up and held it at arms length compressing his lips before he said:

"That's made a b.... of that" and no more. He never sought the miscreant or lost his temper. We had visions of seeing Dub with the cymbals next day.

The following morning we paraded for inspection before joining the head of the column for the day's march. Dub turned up with what looked like a new French horn and calmly fell in line without a word.

"Where did you get that horn?" Tommy asked.

"What horn?" Dub replied "I've always had it."

"Well if that's the same horn how did you get it like that? It was flattened last night."

"You Tommy with all your service should know how to repair an instrument. All I did was bung up the end and give a good blow down it, easy!"

I asked Tommy later what he thought. He said he gave it up. The only explanation was that he must have gone into a nearby copse and taken various twigs and thin branches to poke about and straighten it all out.

"It beats me" Tommy said, "I've seen repairs done before but how he managed that is one of Dub's secrets and he'll never tell."

He never did and he never got another horn. I noticed the valves stuck sometimes but he told me they were only there for ornament really and a good player didn't need them, he used his lip. Now this is true, the lip is most important and Dub had an old horn with no valves, which he had found in a village and he played it until they found him a new one.

There was another occasion when we were marching during very frosty weather with snow on the ground and everything frozen. We had not gone far when we began to lose first one instrument after another with frozen valves. The trombone players nearly lost their teeth bringing the slide up to the top after freeing it from a lower position. Finally we abandoned it altogether and halted. With burning letters supplied by officers and men we thawed out, only to freeze again shortly after. Amongst the brass only one instrument would keep going to the end of a march tune-the French horn could be heard taking up the first cornet part at full blast. It sounded well. Colonel Bogey would have been proud of Dub's performance and 'Sons of the Brave' was the best of all.

Bandsman Kelly was an outstanding man whom I was sorry not to have known longer. He rejoined us as we finished our time round

Kemmel wearing the ribbon of the DCM earned in 1915. I had often heard of him and he was very much liked in the band and elsewhere. He was a regular soldier, a native of Newcastle, tall and well built. He played first cornet magnificently and it was soon evident to me that Tommy and the rest held him in high esteem, not only as a musician but also as a man of sound sense and character.

One Sunday we were holding a special Church Parade, with everyone on parade. It was a fine sight, the band making up the centre of the battalion to lead the hymn singing. Padre Mellish gave out the first hymn: 'Oh God our help in ages past' Punter tapped the stand with his baton and we all played quietly and in good tune for the opening bars then to pause and restart for troops to join in, just as at home. But Tim did not stop, with his eyes to the skies and his chest expanded he carries on 'Our hope for years to come'.... and so on to the end. It sounded lovely as a solo and nothing could stop him. We gradually joined him and the congregation did likewise. Strange looks were exchanged between Punter and Tim and the Colonel and Adjutant didn't look too pleased either.

Once off the parade we heard Punter and Sgt. Carlin wanting to know what he meant by it. He was quite unperturbed.

"I wasn't going to let everyone know I had made a mistake. It was you who were in the wrong in not keeping on with me" Tim said and he stuck to this, like the man whose mother thought he was the only man in step when she saw him for the first time marching as a soldier.

It couldn't have happened in any other band!

CHAPTER FOURTEEN

LEAVE

I left Reninghurst on June 5th for five days leave, having served almost a year in France. With the pass in my pocket, I had to find my own way to Balleul to catch a train for Boulogne. This was quite a distance and I noticed that the enemy was using long distance guns on some cross roads near La Clyte so I made a detour adding another mile but I was taking no chances. The journey was uneventful until I reached King's Cross Station, which was packed with people all fighting to get on the train. There were no seats so we soldiers on leave threw our kits down at the end of the corridor and got our heads down. Later a kindly ticket inspector found us seats but I had a feeling as we passed along the train that we were objects of curiosity. We were dressed in the uniform of the trenches with signs of wear and tear, mud on the equipment we had to carry and trench caps not the smart wire-trimmed caps worn at home.

It was good to see some of my family again after their anxiety about me for twelve months and to check Dad's map on which he had traced my movements and the action at St Eloi very well. It was sad to see the rationing of food and the tasteless black bread they had to eat.

It was more like prison diet, whereas we had at least good white bread in France and continued to have it right until the end. I hoped my ration vouchers for five days would help them but on tendering one for butter and asking for a pound at the Home and Colonial Stores in Briggate I caused a stir.

"A pound" said the young lady, "you can only have two ounces."

"But I'm home for five days" I said.

"Think yourself lucky with two ounces and you can't have any margarine to make it go further." So with that I took my miserable bit of butter and looked forward to a good thick slice well buttered from George when I got back.

Others told me of their feelings when they had been on leave and I felt much the same. There were those who profited from the war and could not care less how long it went on. People who I had thought friends now looked down on me and my like as the PBI. The stories of Private Buttery, Henshaw, Shannon and Day were of no interest to them and they would just say': "Well after all, they did volunteer didn't they? They were not forced to go."

Happily there were others but conscription was too long delayed in my opinion.

My parents said that when I left to go back to France it was as if I was going on holiday with not a care in the world. I loved my parents and my brothers and sisters as they did me but I had no regrets about my service as a volunteer. I was looking forward to going back to my friends who had a duty to do and where I would be happy in spite of the hardships. To me it was the right place to be at that time.

Before I returned I went shopping for presents for my pals as they always brought something back from 'Blighty' so my pack had carried several clay pipes carefully wrapped in wool along with some twist tobacco. No one had ever brought these back before and I was the man of the moment. Smiler, Harry and others were delighted.

Here I ought to say how I became a clay pipe smoker and an addict of twist, which is only for those with a tongue of leather and a capacity for making an abundance of saliva or rather 'spit'. Smiler slept next to me in a barn and it was his custom that wherever he slept his pipe and matches were handy. Having his last puff before settling down he blew a cloud of thick smoke in my face with a chuckle.

"Oh Smiler" I said "Horrible. How do you smoke that stuff? It's like gas."

He laughed and offered me the pipe saying: "Try it yourself. It would do you good and lull you to sleep."

He had a way of persuading people, especially youngsters like me.

"Go on" he insisted "Just one good puff." I took his pipe gingerly and took a pull at the fragrant weed.

"Do you know Smiler, I believe you are right. There is something in that tobacco that no other has. I must get some tomorrow if I can."

So I became a black twist smoker and being where fresh air was in abundance one could smoke it without offence. The satisfaction of twist is for the smoker not the audience. I had to be instructed how to look after a clay pipe, never to entirely clean the bowl as the residue strengthens the refill adding to the potency of the cloud which issues forth.

The long stem is easily broken which produces what the 'Geordie' knows as a 'cuddy'. A good cuddy, especially if well blackened, is the envy of the 'Cuddy Smokers', as they were known north of the Tees. Robinson held the record for keeping and extending the life of his cuddy. Smiler had a habit of placing it under his cap for safety when on the march or parade, providing of course that we were not wearing steel helmets.

During a route march one hot day he had put his pipe in the usual place whilst we played the next march (he always smoked between playing). When the music ended he took off his cap to wipe the perspiration from his forehead then we heard a string of curses coming from the reed section as we marched on. We heard how some 500 feet in army boots would mutilate the best little cuddy he had ever had. When we stopped for a five minute halt at the side of the road, Smiler was reduced to smoking a briar, much to his disgust.

Just then a smart young Officer came up to him and held out his hand

"I think you dropped this some half a mile back my man." He said in a perfect Oxford accent and handed the 'cuddy' back to Smiler intact. Smiler's face was a study as he took it and gave it the most affectionate welcome, almost forgetting to thank the Officer who by now was on his way back to his company. For days we heard: "Now there's a gentleman for you. It's officers like that we ought to have more of and only a kid too. He must have caught it as it was falling. No cuddy could have survived otherwise."

The mystery remained as to how an officer marching behind us managed to rescue a black 'cuddy' of real vintage from being relegated to road grit. As Smiler and his friends agreed "It was bloody marvellous!"

CHAPTER FIFTEEN

THE SOMME

The marching the battalion was doing daily and sometimes at night had a particular purpose. The battle of the Somme opened on July 1st 1916. It was obvious to us that some big move was afoot as we noted the vast amount of guns and equipment moving along the roads and the huge dumps of ammunition. There was an increase in air activity too as the Royal Flying Corps was beginning to equal the numbers of German planes. The sound of gunfire exceeded anything we had heard before and our hopes were lifted, as there now seemed to be no shortage of ammunition. The firing went on day and night and the sky was ablaze. We understood that the battle had opened and that our Division was a flying column ready to go in where the fighting was hardest or danger threatened. The true story of the tragedy of the New Armies being sent in en masse to be cut to ribbons in one day we learned later. We really thought this was the beginning of the end and that at long last the British Army would sweep all before it. By the 10th July we reached the zone of fire and encamped amidst a scene, which was new to us.

The battalion reached 'Happy Valley' but there were no roundabouts or sideshows. As far as the eye could see were signs of war-tents, huts, horses and guns all in a feverish activity and away on the skyline a constant roar of guns, bursting shells and smoke by day and hell's fire at night.

Although it was clear that all this was known and seen by the enemy, life went on regardless. The occasional shell burst in someone's camp or horse lines. Ambulances both horse and motor, threaded their way amongst us as we settled down round George's kitchen for a meal. At night we followed a working party taking up supplies and any casualties they had were our concern.

Gradually it became known that we had a particular job to do. We heard talk of Delville Wood and heavy fighting there and that the position was very fluid. The trenches around us were unoccupied, being but the remnants of our old lines and suitable only for cover. By the 13th we were moved further up to await the final move. Plans had been given to our Officers and senior NCOs and we were to attack Bazentin-le-Petit on the morning of the 14th. Here I must mention an incident, which was often referred to in days to come.

On our many marches during the last weeks, when nearing the actual battle zone during a period between actually playing as a band, we talked amongst ourselves. Tim Kelly said that the night before he had a strange dream. No one talked of dreams unless as a joke but Tim was serious and he was asked about it.

"You all know that we are going into a big battle. It is obvious and it was that which I saw in my dream very vividly." Further enquiries were made.

"Some of us are not going to come back and my dream told me who they were." he said. This became a very serious conversation, no joking. Tim was not the kind of man to play the fool at a time like this.

"Did you see me, Tim?" said Tommy Nichol and asked if he were coming back.

"Yes Tommy" Tim said "You will come back but not as you are going up but you need not be too alarmed. I will tell you that." He volunteered no further information and no one asked for any.

On the 13th we were camped, if it could be called a camp, in the open, surrounded by the activities as mentioned and our companies were preparing to move on. We noticed that Tim was walking up and down deep in thought on his own. Sergeant Carlin went and joined him and they conversed together.

"There's something wrong with Tim, this is not like him at all" was all he said. Even Smiler and Dub, the most sanguine of us all, were worried but I didn't hear anyone refer to his dream.

When darkness fell we moved forward to Caterpillar Valley to establish a dressing station which involved a lot of sandbag work and speed. It must be strong enough to protect the entrance to an old German dugout now facing the enemy lines. There were quite a lot of these in the hillside and one became our billet and George's kitchen.

The valley was under constant very heavy shellfire. This was the site of our own nearest field guns, the heaviest being only some hundred yards behind the front line in places, closer than we had ever been to heavy guns.

Sergeant Carlin told us he had sent Tim to help George in the dugout and that he was worried about him. He had never known Tim like this before.

At daybreak 14th July the barrage lifted and our men went over to take the village from the occupying Germans. The stretcher-bearers were to follow and we left at intervals of one minute knowing that our journey would not be in vain. These journeys were to be numberless as the day went on.

Before my particular stretcher had reached the village we saw Number one coming back but with only two men carrying, Sgt. Carlin and Smiler.

"Who is on the stretcher" we asked "and where is Tim?" We learned that Tim was dead, shot through the throat by a sniper as they were picking up another man. Dixon, the fourth man, had been shot through both legs so they put him on the stretcher and got away. Dixon was a recent recruit to the band. He came from Cleckheaton, was an excellent double-bass player and being a big fellow he had been put to No.1 stretcher. This was a bad start to the day for us and immediately we knew that Tim had known what was to happen.

They gave the stretcher to me and another man with the instructions to go back quickly for the others. The village was now the centre of a bitter battle, which was often hand to hand. The Germans occupied some of the houses still standing, from which they put up a stiff resistance. I learned later that Private Pratt my first pal at Whitley Bay had also been killed. He was going forward in the face of fire to clear a house, which had already cost us dearly, when he was killed outright.

He was now Lance corporal and his section had been held up with casualties but he could not be dissuaded from going forward alone to what was certain death. This was described to me later by men in the section and I thought how like him. He knew no fear at any time.

In 1960 whilst on holiday at Filey I met Dixon and recognised him instantly. He was quite surprised when I approached him:

"Dixon's the name isn't it?" I said.

"Yes, my name is Dixon but you have the advantage of me, although I noticed you gave me a look as you passed me a few minutes ago, as if you knew me."

"Yes I know you. You live in Cleckheaton and the last time I saw you was on July 14th 1916. I carried you out of Bazentin. Cook is my name."

"Cooky!" he said rising up from the seat on the prom, "You are the only man I've ever met from the regiment to this day." He was delighted, telling his wife that this was the man he had often referred to as the one who carried him out. Such meetings are rare and all the more valuable.

By mid morning the scene at the dressing station was pitiable in the extreme, with Captain Gill and Corporal Burns working without a moment's relaxation as we brought in the stream of wounded.

There were no priorities here, as they lay outside in dozens where we put them to await their turn. Those who were known to have no possible chance of recovery had to be put in a nearby dugout to await a merciful death. Captain Mellish and Carlin paid them visits, as they could, no doubt Mellish giving them some comfort, which only such a man could, he too never relaxed. Walking wounded went straight off under their own strength to reach some aid in a back area but many must have died on the way for the whole area was shell ridden.

Caterpillar Valley was a scene fit for any film epic. Guns stood out in the open, even the 9inch howitzers with huge wheels like traction engines. The crews worked ceaselessly loading and firing, paying no heed to the hail of shells seeking them out and bursting all around. The horse driven ammunition columns rode up at full gallop, discharging their load and turning about to bring more still from the rear.

Going about our duties, we were but midgets in the chaos as we made our way to and from the front line disdaining the only cover we had on the way, a sunken road. Over the open took less time and time meant lives. Can men become immune to shellfire? There is no alternative here. One just kept on; there was no time for panic.

Carrying one case down, we had him shoulder high and were making good progress towards the end of our journey when we heard a large shell coming very close indeed. I actually saw it plunge into the ground almost at my feet and then it burst. Four men with a stretcher shoulder high walked out of the black cloud of smoke and hurling metal, unscathed. Not one of us even ducked. As the shell fell I caught a glimpse of Captain Mellish watching us with horror. As we emerged, he ran over to us:

"I saw all that" he said, "I gave you all up. I thought it impossible for anyone to be left but you just walked out like ghosts on your errand. It was a miracle!"

The man on the stretcher was as far as we knew no more affected than the serious wounds he already had and we left him to the tender care of Mellish as we turned back for the next casualty. We managed to make a brief call on George for tea and a quick snack. Carlin was outside the dugout looking very grim and said to us:

"Go inside and sit down for a few minutes rest. You've earned it but don't disturb Smiler. Let him lie quietly. He's had a shock of some sort and I'm very worried about him."

George too looked shocked as he saw our condition. He did a noble job unflinchingly. Tea and food was ready not only for us but many more, even some Indian Cavalry standing nearby with horses, waiting to have the order to advance. This was no place for cavalry. The barbed wire was as bad an enemy and only infantry could hope to penetrate it but at what a cost.

George was also concerned about Smiler. He told us it was serious to see him have to give up. No one could ever imagine such a thing of him. Later we called again and managed to have a word with him, being very careful how we spoke for he was evidently in a state of great emotion.

"What is the matter Smiler?" I asked him.

"I have been out here from the beginning" he answered with tears in his eyes. "Nothing has been too much for me. I don't mind whether a man is still alive or dead I'll bring him out but I don't want another case like the last one." And he broke down again trying to restrain the tears.

Later still we got the full story. He had picked up a very badly wounded man and was carrying him down knowing there was little chance of his survival. They paused to ease his pain and comfort him in some way.

"He began to cry for his Mother" Smiler said between his tears. "That broke me. I could not see that and be unaffected. He was only sixteen and should never have been here at all, poor kid."

Tears are shed at home when bad news comes and anxieties increase but brave men can shed tears too, although they try hard to avoid them. The bravest will tell you that no man is void of fear. It comes to all at some time, only some can suppress it more easily. How true it was.

Smiler returned to duty before the action was over. Carlin was sensible enough to lessen his workload and we felt no grievance as we undertook extra work. Had we had three times the number of stretchers bearers, we would still have been short handed.

To add to our emotional worries, we noticed a tall figure running round in circles alone and in a very exposed place.

"That's Tommy, what is he doing by himself and what's up with him?" we said. "Tommy" I cried running over to him. He was dazed but knew me.

"Tommy, what's the matter?" I asked but I knew he was badly shell-shocked.

"Cooky, where are the others?" he asked me. I told him that all was well and they would be looking for him. He sat down in tears again.

"Those poor lads up there" he said "They cannot go on like this. It's sheer hell, we'll never get them back again and poor Tim, he knew all the time what was going to happen by his dream and yet he went in like the man he was. We'll never see him again."

He got to his feet and I walked him back to hand him over to George, a broken man. He left us to go back to hospital as a shell-shocked case. We were not to see him for some weeks.

The official figures of the casualties to our battalion do not seem to warrant the description I have given but one must remember that we were alongside our brigade friends the 12th West Yorkshire Regiment and the 13th King's Liverpools, both of proven quality in this kind of battle.

There was no priority given to wounded by regiment. If he wanted a stretcher he got one or any other help we could give him. This was a brigade job and the 9th Brigade had a reputation second to none in the 3rd Division noted for its tenacity and always posted where the fighting was thickest.

For five days the struggle went on. The Germans stuck like glue to every bit of trench or cover they had. They had the advantage in that they held the high ground and the houses, or what was left of them.

The Colonel of the Bavarian Regiment who had held the position was eventually taken prisoner along with his staff, some thirty men in a cellar beneath a house, which had withstood everything.

The last night we were there, Smiler and others went up to bring out some German wounded from this cellar. Smiler gave them short shrift, putting the fear of God into them before they were taken away. He had two great hates when I knew him. One was rats and the other Germans. 'Love your enemy' did not apply to Smiler and he had good reason, for he had been a witness in the early days of the war when they used Belgian children as cover from firing in some villages. He had seen enough to warrant his hatred and his recent sympathy for a young lad added to his feelings. He only had to see Germans anywhere to give them a shout of derision and prisoners never escaped the lash of his tongue. To us it was a source of amusement interspersed as it was with Hindustani and a selection of army abuse. To Smiler there were no good Germans, they were all 'Square heads' and their mothers were never married and there were times when I wondered if he wasn't right.

If our politicians had been like Smiler, perhaps there would not have been another war. It says a lot of him that within our five days here he could recover and take up his duties again. In fact I do not think anyone would deny that for sheer guts and hard work, Smiler always led the way.

A stretcher-bearer takes no part in the actual battle apart from his duties to the wounded but he sees what is going on. Captain Carrick, now commanding a company, led an attack of bombers and cleared a house of the enemy taking some seventy prisoners. Little parties of men worked on their own sometimes without an Officer or NCO like the party of Stokes gunners I lay alongside, waiting for a chance to go out to a wounded man. They were held up in a ditch by snipers from a house. They decided to crawl round the back of the house and drop a few mortars through the roof leaving two men to open rifle fire as the occupants tried to escape on this side. We saw the mortar shells ascend and drop through the roof and as the Jerries came out they were dropped like partridges at a shoot.

The Stokes gun was issued to us at Kemmel and was the best reply we had to the German trench mortar. A simple thing invented by a man called Stokes, it was merely a kind of stove pipe some 4feet long on a portable stand. The shell operated when dropped into the muzzle by its own propellant on one end of the shell and exploded on impact. The effect was devastating on open ground and was capable of making a crater some six feet in diameter. The speed of delivery was only limited by the speed at which the gunners could drop the shells into the barrel. This weapon was the forerunner of many but still remained the principal on which the infantry mortars worked. It had the great advantage of being operated by our own crews at will and they became expert with it.

Withdrawal of the brigade on the 19th was to the Divisional Reserve in the region of our old front line prior to July 1st. An area where bivouacs could be built gave the possibility of some sleep although subject to desultory shelling.

Fortunately the weather was fine and we could relax in the sunshine. Bivouacs were made of any material to hand for the whole area was strewn with empty ammunition boxes, discarded waterproof sheets and the flotsam and jetsam of a battlefield. There was no planning of lines; usually two men joined in choosing where to erect their shelter. 'Housey Housey' came into play and to the cries of 'Clickety Click, Kelly's eye' we recovered our nerves and put on weight as we consumed the rations which had been unable to reach us in the last few days.

The artillery columns provided a spectacle unequalled by any circus as they tore up and down over the rolling fields of the Somme. A column of guns and wagons with teams of six horses and mounted drivers was an unforgettable sight. They had to run the gauntlet every day under the surveillance of the enemy balloons. A column would halt in the lea of a trough in the landscape, drivers would dismount to check harness and make adjustments. Then would come the orders "Mount", "Walk march" then as they reached the crown came the cry "Gallop" and off they would go at full stretch with enemy shells at their heels but thank God they got through. Of course it was not always the case as the evidence of shattered wagons, bodies of men and horses waiting burial and the thousands of graves bearing the crest of the Artillery with their motto 'Ubique'-everywhere.

Overhead there was a continuous drone of aircraft and the rattle of machine guns as we looked up to watch a dogfight. To see one shot down in flames reminded us that others faced death often single-handed. We almost became immune to it all and wondered if we would ever pay to go to an air show again, just as we wondered if we could ever want to take part in Guy Fawkes night at home. We had seen it all before.

There were no civilians; this was a man's country. As far as the eye could see they occupied every hole and cranny, trying to snatch a sleep at times to a cacophony which never ceased. Sometimes we might wonder who pays for all the waste, the millions of anti-aircraft shells which burst in white puffs far above usually to no effect as anti-aircraft gunnery is still in its infancy.

The Royal Horse Artillery with their 13 pounders had to use lorries converted for the purpose and when they occasionally hit a target we all cheered. Yet it had some purpose as it kept the German aircraft flying higher than otherwise and rocked him enough to upset his calculations.

There were no skylarks in the blue skies above but the rats survived and were well fed. The lice were still with us too but there is no time to rid ourselves of them and no facilities for a bath as yet.

The truth of the tragedy of July 1st when thousands of men fell in one day had not yet reached us. We were under the impression that this really was going to get us moving and possibly speed the day of peace. We looked towards Albert to see the Cathedral spire still standing with the Virgin lying at right angles hanging by a steel thread. It was thought that this was an omen and that she would not fall until the war was over.

About this time I received a letter from home to tell me that Jack my eldest brother had been wounded in this first day attack and was being sent to England. Later I learned that he had been shot through the body almost immediately he left the trench, the bullet missing his spine by a fraction of an inch, yet he walked down to the first aid post alone. It was not expected that he would ever be A1 again but such was his strength that he later returned to take part with his battalion in future battles. He served in the York and Lancs 9th Battalion.

It was known that the 7th Brigade of our Division fiercely contested the ground we had taken and we were to be transferred to that brigade for a special job. With our friends the 12th W. Yorks and the 13th Kings we were destined for Longueval on the right of Bazentin in Delville Wood.

This was timed for July 23rd and proved as tough a job as Bazentin had been. The village again lay just over the crest of the undulating ground, HQ being further forward than usual and our dressing station in a sunken road named Pont Street, which was actually the jumping off point for the attack. This was no dugout, merely a cut in the side of the road, entirely open to the elements and very close to the firing line, even after the attack had gone forward.

I remember someone said to me:

"Cook you used to grumble at trench warfare and say you would like to meet Jerry round the houses. Well here's your chance, there are houses here." It was true but Jerry occupied them and as he was often in the defensive position, he took some shifting.

If there was one advantage to being a stretcher-bearer, it was that the distance to carry was less but it involved crossing a small hillock within fire from everything. Whizz-bangs opened up immediately we reached the top and against the skyline we were sitting ducks. We devised a drill to pause before actually coming into view and prepare for a sprint. The man on the stretcher was secured and if able we told him to hold tight, then up and over to beat the shells by fractions of seconds and we were in. The dressing station was very close indeed and each journey took us right into the village, picking up men just where they had fallen within yards of the enemy.

Mick Creighton went even further, going into no-man's land to pick up out of a shell hole, a most dangerous thing to do for he was in yards of the muzzles of the enemy rifles. Whether they gave him consideration or not seeing he was wearing an SB brassard is doubtful. They had not done this at Bazentin but Mick picked up his man over his shoulder and made his way in safety. He arrived to meet the Brigadier General Potter who had seen his actions. He asked his name:

"Drummer Creighton, Sir" he was told.

We all felt he had earned a decoration, which would have been well deserved, as he had no thought but to save a man's life. However not a word was heard from official quarters and although he never complained, we were all disappointed.

There was a part of the sunken road, which was very close to the actual firing line. It was pitted with small funk holes dug into the side and provided good cover for seconds but no more. We found a man sitting there with his leg hanging on by a thread, calmly looking at the protruding bone and torn flesh. I knew him immediately; his name was

Cutler. We had nicknamed him Mary in the platoon, as he was a simple fellow certainly out of his element as a soldier.

"Hello Cutler" I said, crouching down beside him, "Got a Blighty one, old man?"

He looked up, recognising me but with a blank look on his face as if he did not realise how serious this was.

"Come on old man. We'll have you away safely in minutes."
He was gently lifted on to the stretcher and with care his leg too but a sliver of skin only attached it. We had to cross the pimple with him and if he was to have any chance of survival it could only be with immediate medical attention. We made it and asked the doctor to give him priority, which he did at once. There was never any mention of him in casualty lists so what happened to him we never knew. I was quite sure that any other in his condition would not survive. Could it be that with his slow intellect he had something others didn't have? He certainly showed no sign of shock and had no idea how serious his injuries were. His quietness was always part of him and he seldom spoke to anyone. What his past was, no one knew but we all felt genuinely sorry for 'poor old Mary', a lonely man.

It became obvious that something was going wrong in this battle. The flanks were not making any progress and the enemy guns pinned us down with concentrated heavy shelling and machine gun fire but we held on for two days. There was no shelter for us here except funk holes in the side of the road. George was no less free from shells than we were when he tried to make tea.

The relief was to be by night and our instructions were that until we received word that all our men were clear, we had to remain where we were. This in itself became a trial as the shelling moved to the road. It became heavier still and to add to this a large ammunition dump close by was hit and we got the contents as it blazed and exploded.

In addition, such a blaze drew more fire from 'over the road'. An Officer, most likely artillery, was working alone trying to remove boxes of ammunition to safety, right in the middle of it, regardless of the danger. We watched spellbound. Finally there was a huge explosion and we saw no more of him. Captain Gill saw this with us as he was waiting for relief under whatever cover we could find. The dressing station was packed up ready to move and no casualties could possibly get in under fire so close. He said he would try to find out who that officer was but he will be one of those 'with no known grave' nor would there have been any remains to bury. This was the most frightening experience we ever had before or since, unable to move, with no cover and the possibility of a direct hit at any time.

Smiler and I shared a small funk hole, if it was worthy of the name and he struck every match he had, trying to keep his cuddy going. Finally he cadged a lighter that I had and wore it out completely! Not being given to swearing, when a shell burst very close and we crouched into even less space, I must have remarked.

"Oh dear! That was close" several times. This was to become a joke to Smiler for weeks to come. Seeing a place with funk holes like those on the Somme, he would point them out to me and say "Cooky-oh dear!" I knew what he meant and I knew he had told the tale to the others that even under these circumstances, Cooky was still a 'By Jove' fellow.

Eventually after what seemed to be hours, the runner came with the news that all the companies were out and clear, so now it was up to us. Captain Gill suggested we make a dash for it in pairs down the road and meet at a spot we all knew where there was shelter. I saw Smiler with his long legs running down that road beside me when a Verey light from the dump flew our way and passed within inches of his face but he never saw it.

Once we arrived in comparative safety a check was made and we found we were one man short.... No George! No one had seen him for some time and no one had any idea where he could be. Captain Gill thought someone should go back to find him. We could not leave him like that. He asked for a volunteer. There was silence...but only for a minute as Smiler said:

"Same old faces. It always falls on to the same men, I'll be off." I could not let Smiler go alone and asked if I could go with him. It was agreed as being a better plan, there being a possibility that one of us at least would get back. We were to return to the little area where we had been, shout his name and if there was no reply after a minute to leave as the position was too dangerous for more. It was good to be with Smiler on this mission. He knew exactly what to do, although it was like going into a blazing house as the dump was well alight by now.

"George, George!" we shouted above the din and then we heard a small voice say:

"I'm here, where are the others?"

He was almost at our feet. It was a wonder we had not fallen into his hole in the ground. We dropped down beside him, a terrified look on his little face beneath his tin hat and only his head and shoulders were above ground. A dud shell could have made the hole. He was scared and could not imagine anyone passing that dump.

"Come on you little...." Smiler said, "Get hold of his hand Cooky and we'll run his legs off." Well we didn't run his legs off but to say they never touched the ground would be nearer the truth as he finally reached safety.

This story has the same sequel as at St Eloi. The Adjutant Captain Pease came to see me next day to tell me I was unlucky. Awards had been allotted to the battalion for gallantry and the Colonel asked all Officers to report incidents they thought worthy. Captain Gill reported the rescue of George, which Captain Pease said was worth at least the Military Medal. However Colonel Wild said, whilst he would like to make an award to stretcher-bearers, as McQuade already had the Military Medal he did not want to make him a second award yet, and as Cook and he were both equally involved it would be wrong to give Cook alone a medal.

"I have to tell you that you are unlucky" the Adjutant said again "and I am very sorry but thought you ought to know." He was exceeding his duty a little in doing this. I don't think the Colonel would have been pleased had he known but Captain Pease as I have already said, was one in a thousand. He himself earned the MC and served the battalion until September 1917 when he transferred to the Royal Flying Corps.

Again I say that this did not worry me in the least, it was sufficient to have been there and come back alive. 'A dead dog is better than a live lion.' Why Captain Gill was not given an award was a mystery. If ever a man earned one he did.

Whilst not in any way decrying awards for men of real merit the system was rotten somewhere. This was proved when a DCM was given to a Sergeant Cook co-incidental to his making sausages, having for the first time received a barrel of sausage skins bought out of mess funds and used for the men as a gift to supplement his rotten stew. Smiler who knew this individual very well and had a poor opinion of him often referred to this. It was always quoted when he was checked for not wearing his ribbons.

"Military Medals" he would say "Kutch! They are given for making sausages." Kutch being the Hindustani word for No, a very expressive way of saying it.

Too few medals were given to men in the ranks and too many are worn by Officers who never even had to duck. The excuse that an Officer wears his medal for his company does not hold water in many cases but this is not to say that many were not well earned. I had a friend with a VC and he held the same view. I have no doubt he earned his medal but he never thought his action equal to others who never got a mention. To me it was sufficient that I earned the respect of Smiler and others which was worth much more than any medal.

CHAPTER SIXTEEN

LONELY TRENCH

The Third Division had been heavily engaged and was due for a rest and reinforcements. Histories tell us that they were some 3,000 men short following the recent fighting, so we moved back on July 26th, first to Albert where we now saw the devastation of that beautiful city. We saw the Virgin statue again still lying at right angles to the cathedral spire. It resembled Ypres, a mere shell of a town.

Two days later we moved back to better billets at Ville-sur-Ancre. Here we were able to tidy ourselves up and reform as a band. George was able to set up his kitchen and meals were once again up to his best standard and he looked happy having recovered from his fright. Smiler too was back on form but we had for the time being lost Tommy. We were able to find newcomers with band experience and we gained Gilbert, a young man from the Midlands who was a very good cornet player and as his second, Bradshaw. Both had been in Colliery bands. Private Larkins was an old reservist called back to the colours and was a valuable addition as he could play the euphonium until we had Tommy back.

Tommy was missed very much. He was slightly deaf or at least he said so. He had a pleasant cultured voice and impressed us with his superior knowledge of politics, soldiering and music. He had a tendency to let the euphonium rip especially in a march tune, where his rendering of the counter melody in 'Old Comrades' or 'Colonel Bogey' was superb. Punter dared to restrain him at practice, to which Tommy replied:

"The euphonium is a very noble instrument. It is intended by its tone to be heard above all other instruments in the band even in the most delicate passages. I use it as it was intended." With that we resumed our rendering of 'La Paloma'!

Smiler's oboe had seen better days, yet he played it beautifully, although it was under constant repair in his spare moments. Having a key missing, he had bunged up the hole with clay or 'mutti' as he used to say. We were playing in the open to the officers and men who were at ease around us. All went well until we came to the item 'The Chocolate Soldier'. Smiler's oboe solo was going well until he reached the high note. Instead of the note we expected came an exasperated "A tour-a-mutti Munster" which being interpreted, if my Hindi is anywhere near correct, is 'A little mud mister'. His bit of clay had dropped out of the hole and no sound was heard when he tried the high note. After this remark he calmly went on and finished the solo and we took our cue from the bandmaster and continued.

To laugh on parade would have been equal to dropping a rifle on the King's Birthday Parade. The laughter came later when we were dismissed and although Punter suggested we try to get him another oboe he refused saying his was an instrument matured by age. He didn't like new ones they were like clay pipes, they needed seasoning and the war wouldn't last that long.

Such were the lighter sides of soldiering as when we were billeted in a barn, very comfortable, nice and dry with plenty of good straw. Unfortunately it was alive with rats as witnessed by a dog we had acquired somehow, which we encouraged in rat hunting. At night we had settled down and lights were out when we heard a rustling and then a yell. Immediately candles were lit again and all was confusion. A large rat had fallen down from a beam on to Smiler's face. We were just in time to see it dash across the straw and under Cassidy's blankets at his feet. Cassidy, our Provost Sergeant, was sharing our billet with his men at the time. He leapt out his bed in his shirt giving us all a good view of his long skinny legs and his policeman's feet as he fairly danced, the rat being as scared as he was.

It was a long time before we got to sleep for laughing and the more we laughed the more Cassidy got annoyed. We had visions of being arrested for some trivial matter after this. His professional pride had been wounded. In the morning our canine friend caught what we assumed to be the same rat in the hollow of a wall. It was the biggest rat I ever saw. Smiler, as I said had a hatred of rats second only to Germans and this was indeed a shocking thing to happen to him. He didn't laugh, he trembled at the thought and cursed all rats back to Hamelin.

These were just interludes, the battle of the Somme still went on and we had another role to play. The reinforcements arrived, some returning from hospital and we had a new General for the Division, General C. Deverall.

Our task this time was to relieve pressure on the area we had already been in at Delville Wood and to take a position known locally as 'Lonely trench'. Several units had tried this but they had failed.

Prior to taking up position, we moved closer and took part in some very big night fatigues, carrying ammunition and engineering supplies, in which we lost some men. We began to see that the new drafts had men who were what we termed Lord Derby's men, conscripts not as good as the volunteer army had been. Lord Derby had been instrumental in bringing in a bill for conscription at home and older men were drawn in too.

Eventually we relieved the troops in position by daylight, as the communication trenches gave good cover and there was a deep valley and road parallel to the firing line as at Caterpillar Valley. Disaster struck us immediately for we had not taken our equipment off nor unloaded medical supplies before there was a cry for stretcher-bearers. The signallers had taken a direct hit into their dugout nearby and had casualties to be evacuated. The valley was under fire from three directions by enemy guns and there was no cover under these circumstances. No sooner had we taken over our own billet from the King's stretcher-bearers than the shelling came nearer.

A large projectile, evidently from a long distance gun, whizzed over our heads and dropped in the road taking away the back of a general service wagon. It left the driver like Ben Hur sitting on his high driving seat with only two wheels under him and a team of terrified horses going full stretch down the road. This was such a funny sight we all laughed but someone suggested we get into the dugout as the next shell could be for us. The corporal of the King's was sitting outside finishing his breakfast and refused to come in, feeling quite safe. Immediately we heard it as it fell, just as anticipated, on the place where we had been standing. In fact we had not all got in before we heard the terrific explosion and force of it threw us back into the doorway as we all tried to get in at once. No one was hurt but we wasted no time in seeking the Corporal. There was no Corporal, only a shell hole and the remains of cooking utensils. This was indeed a bad start as we knew him well and respected him. He had worked with us before. It was almost as bad as the loss of Tim at Bazentin.

Meanwhile the companies had their troubles for they came under fire in the communication trench and casualties began to pour in, both walking wounded and shell-shocked. The latter were from the new drafts, obviously this was their baptism of fire and they could not take it. We simply told them to keep going and they went back out of it. Going to pick up wounded I met Ginger Garland coming down the trench full of smiles.

"Hello Cooky" he said, "I've got a Blighty one at last. It's taken a long time lad but it's sure this time."

His arm was shattered from shoulder to elbow but he wouldn't stop at our Dressing Post and said he would get to the Field Ambulance on his own. So I lost another old friend and the battalion lost a man as good as three of these new blokes, I thought. I was already losing patience with them as they refused to go further towards the front line. Had they seen what we were later to see they would have been even less inclined.

It was difficult to see what was going on as the communication trench was very narrow and progress very difficult. We learned later that several daylight attacks had been made on Lonely Trench and many lives lost adding to the bodies of the West Yorks and others who had been trying to take it for days.

Darkness had fallen before we were able to get right up, knowing there were many wounded to bring down. They had made an assembly trench ready for the next effort, very narrow and shallow. As we made our way along it looked to me that these fellows crouched down were the men waiting to attack and I shook them saying:

"Make way, stretcher-bearers" but there was no response. Then I realised these were dead men from an earlier attack. They lay in dozens.

All night we spent back and forward to take those who had a chance, walking over dead bodies as we carried our loads. Meanwhile the fight went on close at hand. There was no let up at all. It was sheer hell.

We lost Cosh Hill that night. He had disappeared somewhere and in daylight a search was made of every nook and cranny of the trenches but no Cosh. Some West Yorkshire lads who were still there although they should have gone out with the relief, told Sgt. Carlin that they had seen a man going towards the German trench with a rum jar in his hand. He had no rifle but they had seen some kind of band round his arm. He was shouting: "Fix Bayonets! Charge!" They thought he was someone demented by shell shock. They didn't see him fall.

Further enquiries elicited the information that jars of rum had been found lying about somewhere and we came to the conclusion that Cosh had found one and the inevitable happened. We gave him up for dead surely.

Weeks later Sgt. Carlin had a letter from Cosh's mother saying they had a letter from him. He was a prisoner of war in Germany and he wanted them to know he was alright. There was relief all round as we discussed the scene of Cosh arriving amongst Germans, drunk to the eyeballs, and talking twenty to the dozen as he could when under the influence. There must be some good Germans or Cosh would have been shot at sight. We liked to think they had a good laugh at him. They deserved it!

Official records of this battle pay tribute to the German garrison of Lonely Trench. It was perfectly sited with machine guns that could rake the opposing forces and only by a very heavy and concentrated barrage could anyone hope to overcome them. Records say that it cost the Fifth Battalion 200 casualties including Captain Glyn RAMC who suffered shell shock and although another doctor replaced him immediately we missed him.

Our relief could not come too soon. We moved back to near Happy Valley to prepare for rest. Our only happiness was that we were out of Guillemont and received the largest allowance of rations we had ever seen. The supplies had come for the whole battalion but with two hundred not there to receive them, we tucked in. George was delighted to have a joint to roast and vegetables in abundance. Pork and beans we disdained as also Fray Bentos Corned Beef, but it was a sad thought that we had lost so many friends and we felt the best of the regiment had gone with them. At Happy Valley our tent was pitched close to an 18 inch gun mounted on a railway truck, the first we had seen. When it fired it rolled back some hundred yards and when it had finished its quota it left along with its crew. We expected reprisals but fortunately escaped them. We had seen it on the first day but the first time it fired we were in bed and it lit up the tent and the roar shook the lot of us. It was like St Eloi all over again with the mines going up. However railways have other uses and we were soon boarding the train and moving on again.

CHAPTER SEVENTEEN

TRAVELLING MINSTRELS

The label on the carriage said '40 Hommes 8 Chevaux' but as the band and stretcher-bearers numbered only twenty in all we had room to spread our legs. We travelled 'premier classe' being of great importance, anticipating numerous concerts for the troops and the Officers Mess.

Upholstered seats were not provided on this train and the previous passengers had left their mark in the carriages with numerous hoof marks and the smell of manure lingering on the floorboards. Who cared! It was better than Shank's Pony and we all learned the technique on making tea at the engine, unless George could devise a means of boiling a dixie, which he did. The engine supplied the coal and a convenient oil drum the fireplace.

It was cold at night and we kept the fire going, although we had no chimney but smoke rises so men lying on the floor could breath comfortably. In the morning the train stopped for the battalion to have breakfast When the doors were opened and we got out we were like the Kentucky Minstrels with smoke blackened faces and the comments were hilarious. Our truck was the only one with a coal fire and we stood out like chapel hat pegs from the other troops. The hot water could not reach us fast enough as we stripped and washed the soot away. As to our clothes, well we could only hope they would wear clean or a kind Quartermaster would take pity on us, being the Regimental Band.

Travelling by troop train in France can be quite amusing and whilst other units may have found it rough, to the infantryman, especially after being in the trenches and poor billets, it can be luxury. For one thing discipline is relaxed to the extent that each van is a unit of its own and close pals usually get together. The NCOs forgot their superiority for once if they had any sense. The men respect their rank but they would be expected to 'muck in' with whatever is going in rations or recreation. Rations would be poor, mostly bully beef and biscuits. Bully was in such good supply that we found a new use for it.

As the train approached a level crossing one could hear plaintive 'Bully Beef! Biscuits!' from children and others who knew that a troop train was manna from heaven. The troops were generous even if unusual in the method of dropping the food. Opening the van doors to full extent the 'bombers' would stand, poised, their ammunition at their feet. On reaching the target (the crossing gate) over went a shower of Bully Beef in unopened tins, jam and biscuits which flew like cardboard in the wind and the scramble of the kids to pick it up was worth seeing. I only once saw what might have been a calamity but the train did not stop to let us investigate fully as it 'raced' on at 10mph. Amongst the missiles was a 7lb tin of Fray Bentos, which hurtled like a trench mortar to drop on an old man, one of the scramblers. I don't think he was hurt seriously but it bowled him over.

The band settled down well to its enforced idleness en-route being inveterate card players. In order of preference the games were Halfpenny Nap, Solo preferably with a kitty, Brag (most favoured but likely to break friendships) and finally Spoof, otherwise known as dominoes with cards. This was the last resort and played when we were hard up prior to payday, as one could play for hours for a penny, which changed hands frequently. It was also the worst game for starting an argument for they were all expert players and to play a card out of sequence was a crime. More laughs came from 'Spoof' than any other card game. Of course for the more serious minded there was Cribbage, a game I never mastered. Smiler and Larkins were the real devotees. 'One for his hat' or 'one for his knob' was the expression, used in deep and serious tones but I never understood the real satisfaction they seemed to get from it. Nobody boasted of his winnings in the 'school' as everything came back to us later. The winner would be the one to stand the drinks at the next estaminet or a bottle of wine would go round the billet. I know I never suffered from whatever I lost by the fickle 'Lady luck'.

On one occasion we arrived at a large railhead, disembarked and the battalion was forming up in column ready to march off with the band at the head. It happened that we formed the band's ranks immediately behind a large army truck carrying black troops, probably from East or West Africa. They were naturally drawn to the sight of a band with gleaming brass instruments to the fore. One face stood out with a grin from ear to ear and eyes like shining saucers as he raised his hands towards us palms outspread and cried:

"Oh! De music am good and de 'ambone am sweet!"

Of course our dignity would not allow us to reply being on parade, but I often heard it repeated to me as I played my part as a trombonist at subsequent performances.

The official historian of the Regiment makes mention of the loss on the Somme of many of our best men and seasoned troops and the lack of experience of the new drafts which were sent out to reinforce us. During the next few weeks we moved from camp to camp and away from the range of even the long range guns; a very welcome change to all which gave us time to re-organise our shattered ranks. Colonel Wild who had led us at St Eloi and Bazentin and Guillemont was given a post in England, there to take up some training duties to which no doubt he would be very useful. Major Herbert, soon to be Colonel Herbert succeeded him. He was welcomed by the old soldiers who had known him from his early days in India as a subaltern and later in France as an Adjutant.

Colonel Herbert was an excellent soldier in all respects. On meeting him, I was struck by his immaculate appearance. He looked the part, a man to be respected and obeyed and always attentive to the comfort and well being of his men. No one was going to pull the wool over his eyes and he missed nothing at inspections. We moved some twenty miles west of Albert and rested at Fienvillers and then on to Bonnieres and Eps, where the companies had training in the field. As Battalion, a Brigade and Division we occasionally took part but generally we were left to our own pursuits involving band practice and playing whenever we could to the troops and the Officers Mess.

No doubt we improved and were always welcome as leaders in the marches. In all it was a very happy time for us. Tommy came back after his spell in hospital looking quite fit and glad to be back once more to take up his euphonium and give us the accent on the counter melodies which Larkins had not the wind for.

After our travels in what might be called a peaceful area we arrived at Marles-Le-Mines near Bruay at the end of August. We were inspected about this time by a high ranking General, some said it was Haig others General Horne. Whoever he was we saw little of him. The parade was timed for early morning and the whole Brigade had to present in review order. This entailed a lot of cleaning and polishing which had not been the practice for some considerable time so we probably looked the worst for wear. To get a crease in trousers men went to the tailor's shop for ironing by the experts. This must have been the heaviest chore they ever had as men lined up in the open, handed over their trousers and stood waiting for the job to be done.

At the crack of dawn our own NCOs and Officers, Adjutant and C.O inspected us, with eagle eyes. Not a button was out of place and boots must be shining with liberal applications of dubbin, the only polish allowed. Then came a long march to a large field where we were lined up in ranks straightened out with absolute precision and much bawling of Sergeant Majors and silent curses by the troops.

So extensive was the area covered that orders could only be obeyed simultaneously by flag, microphones not having been invented by then. This had to be rehearsed. Slope arms, Order arms, Present and so on. Sounds ridiculous!

We all expected that the visitors would at least come through the ranks but no such luck. We might at least have seen his face. Along with his 'brass hats', he arrived by car, transferred to a charger and came on to the field. The band played the General's Salute, as the men Presented Arms, then the visiting cavalcade rode round the perimeter and finished up at the gate to see us all march past.

"Eyes left" gave us a fleeting glance of a 'bloke on a horse'. We saw as much of him as he saw of us but the company lads had a lot to say about marching to attention for a mile or two at the slope, without even a 'change arms' to relieve cramped muscles. So much for General's inspections! They ought to have come to see us at 'Lonely Trench' or Longueval. This may sound a little peevish but to the lower ranks and not professional soldiers, such parades are 'baloney' when they are for the satisfaction of the Top Brass. We would have done it better and with pleasure for our own Officers and our new Colonel.

A much better parade was one we had on St George's Day when we trooped the colours and played a very nice tune whilst the inspection of the lines was going on by the visiting notables along with the colonel. This was a family affair and enjoyed by all ranks. To me there was only one flaw as the tune we played which is often used on such occasions is known as 'May Blossom' and reminded me of another version to which Smiler and Co had other words.

The area around Neoux-le-Mines and Loos were mining areas, reputed at the time to be 'cushy', that is they were not as hectic as the trenches we had been used to at Ypres. We had heard of such places but so far seen little of them and some thought this was no place for us and someone would be sure to start something as we were here. Amongst our new Officers we had some dashing young men, one in particular was a bombing enthusiast and parties went out seeking information and possible prisoners. The Germans were well ensconced in deep dugouts behind the pit hills safe from any artillery fire.

Being a bands-man I was not on this raid but those who took part told the story in detail to me and is quite true. So secure did Fritz think himself that it was soon known that he was not keeping sentries posted too well. Our party went round under cover of darkness and surprised him in his safe retreat by placing a man at each saphead with a Stokes Gun shell in his hands. At a given signal the pins were released and they were hurtled down to the depths with a cry of "Share that amongst you" then they left everyone to get back safely. The effect must have been disastrous and the peace of the community very much disturbed. Other raids brought the prisoners in for identification. Jerry must have known the Northumberland Fusiliers had arrived!

Christmas 1916

The battalion remained in this sector for the remainder of the year. Activities continued with bombing raids, seeking information by the capture of prisoners and in repairing defences. The weather was very bad in that we had an abundance of rain and snow. This made living conditions very difficult but fortunately casualties were light and our work as stretcher-bearers less arduous so we worked on defences and fatigues mostly at night.

Christmas Eve was spent in a wood in a canvas tent rather like a large bivouac but this gave us little shelter from rain, which percolated through the canvas continually, and it was impossible to keep dry. The fire inside was fed by damp wood, which we had collected, and the company had anything but a cheerful Christmas.

The Christmas pudding had arrived and was served to all. This came in a large tin, which was boiled before opening and then with some difficulty spooned out in chunks, still as hard as iron and without either custard or rum sauce. In all it was a miserable crew with little to say to one another.

Dub was the only one to break the long silence. Around us lay an assortment of branches and twigs for fuel. Picking up one, which had a peculiar curve resembling a saxophone, he put it to his lips and said:

"First time I've seen this instrument" which raised a laugh, probably the only laugh of the day. Trust Dub to find something funny, no matter where we were or what the situation.

Christmas Day saw us on the march again to an unknown destination as far as we were concerned, which eventually turned out to be towards Arras. We did manage to lead as a band but under such wintry conditions it was not a great success. We spent a day or two resting and were able to put on a few programmes for the Officers Mess, always enjoyable for us especially if they were billeted in a large house or chateau where we could play indoors.

Early January was bitterly cold and rations were poor too. Some said this was due to enemy activity in the English Channel but more likely to the difficulties of transport, still mainly by horse. Not only did we suffer but the horses and mules too and fatigues often entailed burying them lying stiff and swollen on the roadside. Drivers said they simply dropped dead from exhaustion due to lack of corn.

On reaching the town of Arras we had the luxury of houses and buildings for billets. These still stood, many intact but unoccupied, whilst others still had civilians trying to eke out a living, mainly from the occupying troops.

Stretcher-bearers were allotted a room on the third floor of a large house. Our first thought was to make a fire, for we were all frozen. The room contained furniture, one being a large round table with carved legs. In minutes this provided us with the best fire we had seen for weeks, although it seemed sacrilege to burn such a valuable table. During our stay in the house other pieces went the same way and we started on the floorboards before higher authorities intervened. We took the view that the likelihood of the owners ever returning to find the house intact was a forlorn hope to say the least, as shells fell into the street spasmodically and Arras was gradually disintegrating into rubble.

It was obvious that there were preparations for another big battle as we saw huge dumps of ammunition being made and the movement of guns concentrated on the region of Arras. All our energies were put into this and as usual infantrymen became beasts of burden with carrying parties day and night.

The large number of cellars and underground passages were extended right under the enemy lines. These were fitted out with electric light and light railway tracks, which served to convey spoil from sapper's work which we emptied in the open. These tunnels felt totally secure as they were solid chalk and very deep. One intersection was a huge cave with tunnels leading in several directions. It would have been quite easy to get lost in such a labyrinth of underground works and sentries were placed at points to guide as well as for security. I was on some errand with a companion when we passed a sentry. He was one of few old hands left, a Boer War veteran, Johnny Killoran. A few paces on, my companion said: "Did you smell Johnny's breath?" then we turned back to speak to Johnny. He smelt strongly of rum and we asked him if he had any. Producing his water bottle it was practically full of raw spirit. How Johnny had found rum down there we never learned but trust him to get it if it was available. Obviously he had found a store and his duty was a happy one.

For several nights fatigues consisted of laying a cable which had to be dug in to a depth of two feet. The ground was frozen and it was the hardest work possible as we broke picks and shovels on the rock-like earth and each night we took extra tools to replace the ones we knew would be broken. On completion of this job we moved back to Berlencourt 16 miles back to train for the battle to come.

As we marched out of Arras in companies, the Colonel stood to see us as we passed taking the salute by platoons. It was very smartly done considering our state but there was one fault in the ranks. A man was seen to be supported by two others endeavouring to keep him upright and escape the eye of the CO. No such luck! It was Johnny Killoran, evidently still under the influence of rum with his feet trailing helplessly as he was literally carried along.

"Fallout that man" came the order and seeing his condition.

"Put him on the transport." Nothing missed Colonel Herbert.

Next morning Johnny was before the CO at his orderly room and what took place was a tribute to Colonel Herbert's understanding of men.

"Killoran" he said "I've been looking up your records. I see you are the oldest soldier in the battalion. You have been here since August 1914 and you have never missed a trio into the trenches. You have never been wounded nor ever in hospital for any reason. You are a good soldier but you have one fault: DRINK!" he continued:

"I have decided that you need a change and in future you will do duty with the water cart."

We were highly amused at the idea of Johnny being in charge of water instead of rum. The duties of the water cart personnel were very important, ensuring that the water was fit for consumption, cooking and drinking. In a country with so little naturally clean and drinkable water meant the addition of chlorine which we had already come to accept. We all turned out next morning to see Johnny at his new duties, following the cart on foot to the filling point. He gave us all a knowing wink and was no doubt going to be good at his job and he had earned a rest from more dangerous duties.

Although the battalion had been made up to strength there were many of the new men who lacked experience of trench warfare and it was decided to strengthen the companies with men who had served a longer period in France although not actually combatants. The stretcher-bearers were to be replaced by men from the companies and for the time being we were to take up our rifles and return to our old companies. The men I had known in X Company were nearly all gone mostly as casualties. Although it seemed an unusual move to take us from the work we had done for so long, especially on the Somme, we took it in our stride knowing that when we came back from the line we would regroup as a band again.

We did eventually take up our old duties again but it was to be longer than we anticipated.

The Germans had been quiet on this particular front lately. Taking over the front line trenches in daylight was an unusual experience but communication trenches ran right up from the town itself and were quite safe. The troops we relieved said they had been here for a week without any casualties. Before we had settled in we were told to get ready to go over the top, the Germans having relinquished their front line, according to reconnaissance patrols.

There was to be no preliminary bombardment, we would just walk in. It sounded too good to be true but so it turned out as we moved over with fixed bayonets.

Jerry had left his line but not before completely destroying all dugouts and parapets. The trench was merely a wide ditch and very wet. We found that they had built a barricade, which they still held so our first task was to flush them out. This fell to our platoon and the plan was to take up positions and allow a party of bombers under Lieutenant Hadow to go behind the blockade. They would engage the Germans, who we expected to try to escape our way, and we would have them on a plate. This sounded alright but things seldom go as expected and anything could happen. Lieutenant Thorpe was a new Officer to me; a former clergyman now turned combatant and very daring. He and Hadow had worked together before and made a good pair.

Thorpe led us along and quietly placed each man in position, singly, with a few yards between him. I was the last to be placed a few yards from the German barricade with very little cover. With my rifle in position and my two bombs handy, Thorpe whispered to me:

"When you hear Mr Hadow and his party throw their bombs be ready for Jerry coming this way. Open fire immediately and we will come forward to you." Then he crept away along the trench leaving me alone. I thought I had little chance of survival but I should at least try to drop someone before being over-run, which seemed a certainty. All seemed very quiet as I lay there waiting Eventually someone crept up behind me. It was Lieutenant Thorpe.

"Come back Cook, It's all off." Was I relieved! Apparently the plan had reached HQ who thought it was of no purpose and too risky for the sake of a few men who could stay there for what harm they were doing. They were isolated from their own lines as it was.

Discussing this with others as we gathered together later we were joined by Sammy Somersgill. Sammy was about the only man I knew in the company now. He had been in the platoon for a long time and was an old hand. I asked him where he had been and if I thought I had had an experience, he had worse.

Lieutenant Hadow had discovered a tunnel with sappers working in it. It was known that the Germans were also tunnelling close by and had been heard working. Sammy was placed at the extreme end of it with a revolver and several boxes of high explosive with instructions that should he hear any movement of the German sappers he was to fire into the boxes. It was likely that once our attack on top had started they would blow their own sap sky high to catch us. Sammy had been alone for about an hour, sitting in total darkness with ears strained, knowing full well that he would commit suicide doing his duty. Sammy was just the fellow to do this but we were glad it never took place, for he was a married man. Normally he would not have been picked for that reason but I doubt if any of the other men would have stayed as he did.

Lieutenant Thorpe took me as his runner and I was to see more of him. I liked him but thought he was just a bit 'green', taking risks unnecessarily at times in his enthusiasm. One night we were in the open, patrolling when a mist came up. In such situations everything becomes an enemy and he touched my arm to halt, peering through the mist at something he was sure was a man. He was preparing to fire until I told him it was a barbed wire stake and not to rouse all the sentries in the neighbourhood, who would certainly have opened up on us.

I was appointed as his runner and the accent was on running. I never saw a more enthusiastic Officer before. He simply raced from one point to another; his enthusiasm for war knew no bounds. Eventually he made the error I had anticipated for him. When challenged by a sentry in total darkness, he failed to reply immediately and the sentry quite rightly pointed his bayonet at him and caught him in the throat. He would survive but it meant him leaving us for hospital treatment but not without first apologising to the sentry and absolving him from blame. In fact he congratulated him on being a very vigilant and efficient soldier. He never came back to the battalion but no doubt he would make his mark elsewhere.

We continued to hold this part of the line but conditions became even worse with continuous rain and no efforts of ours could make even a semblance of a trench nor any kind of shelter. The enemy sent over shell-fire and some mortars, which gave us a rough idea of their position. Our patrols were able to add to this, one even penetrating their line and reaching a battery of 88mm's firing from a copse, they stood watching for a few moments then silently returned to our lines.

We held on here for five days until one morning a party of Germans was seen coming towards us, evidently intent on a raid. We opened fire on what was really an easy target as they bunched together but after a night of heavy rain and the resultant mud, the rifles were soon useless. Mine stuck after four rounds and to open the bolt I had to kick the bolt back with my boot. The Lewis gun, which could have decimated the whole enemy party, stuck after half a pannier, so now we anticipated a much closer combat with bayonets but Jerry thought better of his enterprise and turned tail, rather to our disgust. In spite of everything we could have made a good account of ourselves aided by some Canadian sappers who had come from below on hearing the noise.

Rifles were always kept in good working order. I never saw one fail before but these conditions made it impossible to avoid. Eventually we were relieved and went back to our former billets there to clean up and make up for the sleep we had lost. There followed another week of heavy fatigues, digging trenches at night and carrying materials up from the rear dump. One night we carried a cargo of cylinders, some five feet long, for a special detachment of Royal Engineers. Each cylinder was suspended on a pole and two men shouldered it along in a column, Chinese fashion. Being a very dark night and in the haste to move away from the dump our fears grew, as we encountered shellfire we felt that if a cylinder was hit we should all be gassed. Now and then we halted to change shoulders for they were very heavy and in retrospect it was funny to see two men lying across the cylinder to prevent it being hit by flying shrapnel, preferring wounds to themselves rather than to see the party gassed.

On reaching the front line we handed our loads to the waiting Engineers who had prepared holes in the parados into which we dropped the cylinders. To our surprise, not one of the fifty men had noticed that the cylinders were empty, one end being an open aperture. I never discovered what these things actually did but evidently had something to do with liquid fire for later in the big attack the German front line became a furnace of flame.

Carrying shells for the Artillery also fell to us. We carried them with great care as if they were eggs only to see the artillerymen sling them into a wagon for further use. When we questioned them they laughed saying they had no detonators as yet. Nevertheless we preferred carrying sandbags or duckboards which we were more familiar with.

It was obvious that the big push was near as guns stood ready everywhere and shells stacked in profusion beside them. At last we seemed to have shells to spare. We thought back to the days at Ypres in 1915 when our batteries counted the rounds and were strictly rationed.

Again I was fortunate. Following a new policy it was decided by higher command that in the coming battle where casualties might be heavy, some of the older experienced men and some Officers should be kept back in the opening stages to strengthen the survivors, who would be new to these conditions. The stretcher-bearers were included as we all had a long experience in the line and had all been combatants too. Men were taken from the companies to take our place as bearers but with no previous training. We doubted the advisability of this, although we had no say in the matter. The army does not let men be idle and we were allotted duties behind the lines. We were sent to the village of Warlus some three miles from Arras, there to become sanitary men keeping the village clean, as this was the forward headquarters of the Corps, complete with the General and his staff.

The billet given us was a good one in an old farm building. We had no objections as we had George to do our cooking and rations drawn direct from the divisional dump. We were under the orders of the Town Mayor who we never saw but he had delegated a little RAMC corporal trained in sanitary work. He was a good fellow but a bit of a joke as he worked to the book in everything and we had to learn from him. I was deputed to be in charge of the incinerator, learning to keep the fire going with old tins and waste paper that we had in abundance. When there was a really good blaze, I threw the contents of the latrine buckets on it, keeping to windward as the stench could be nauseating in the extreme. Also I had a lot of old smoke bombs to dispose of. I also took part in street sweeping with others, leaning on the brush as troops and transport passed by with looks of envy at men with a 'cushy' job. On the Somme we had once passed a Guards regiment doing the same job and it was probably due to such that we avoided a plague.

Probably the most unpleasant job was to bury the numerous horses and mules lying in and around Warlus, their bodies swollen and decomposing. Here our corporal gave us a lecture how, according to army regulations such bodies had to be buried in a hole six feet deep and to speed decontamination the body should be slit open before covering with earth. The first one lay not far from our billet in what we considered virgin soil, another necessity according to our instructor. He measured out the hole in case we skimped the job and once satisfied he left us to the burial. It was safely rolled in and standing around we debated who was to be the butcher...No volunteers, not even to lend a Jack –knife for the job.

"Oh, come on let's get the job done" I said, "if we stick a pick into it that should do", but still they stood around as if waiting for the burial service.

"In for a penny in for a pound" I said jumping into the hole with a pick in my hands. Standing on that poor horse was like standing on a feather bed as I lifted the pick and aimed at what I thought to be its intestines. Horsehide was tougher than I thought and it took a really good swipe to penetrate but I sank it in up to the shaft. Taking the pick out released the gases and the effluvium sent my mates running, leaving me to climb out of the hole alone which I did like lightening. On reaching my friends no one wanted to know me.

"Cooky, you stink" they said, which added insult to injury. However they did go back to fill in the grave and meanwhile I went for a walk to clear the smell, which certainly clung, but I was not fit company at a meal and my appetite suffered.

Volunteering for fatigues can be risky at times. Usually the volunteer hopes it will lead him to a cushy billet or to miss a parade. Like many more I took my chances sometimes only to learn that 'fools venture where angels fear to trend'. On one occasion the Officers Mess had bought a pig and there was a request for any one with butchering experience to report to the battalion butcher. This sounded an easy one so with two others I reported for duty saying I had once worked for a butcher. I had actually delivered orders for three successive Saturdays for the butcher my brother was apprenticed to in Middlesborough. Apart from handing out sausages or chops to customers I knew nothing of the business.

Led by the Corporal of the butcher's department a party of six went to collect a pig from a neighbouring farm and transport it live on a Maltese cart. It was the largest sow I had ever seen lying in a sty which had not been cleaned for weeks. Six pairs of hands and arms linked beneath the animal lifted it into the cart but that pig had no intention of staying there and immediately scrambled back to earth. It took refuge in the village pond, stirring up the dirt and refuse of ages. By now we had an audience of villagers and troops with advice as to how to recover a stray pig but no volunteers to go in and bring it out. By a fuselage of stones and much shouting, it eventually came out, now an even worse sight and very slimy for us to lift into the cart again. This time we managed to get a rope across its back not before it nearly hung itself in its efforts to escape, squealing as only a pig can. The return journey to camp was achieved by walking alongside and hanging on to the rope, with myself hanging on to its tail, which was anything but a secure hold. Finally we delivered it to the slaughterhouse where a felling axe despatched our pig. Once again I returned to my friends who told me I stank and I vowed not to volunteer again, a vow I broke several times. Volunteering must be in my blood.

Warlus provided us with a lot of fun, if nothing else, besides being a cushy billet. Rations were brought from the dump and were very liberal and we even got strawberry jam and delicacies, which never reached us when in the line. Two men were delegated to go with the driver and present the authorising chit. Mick Creighton and I had this duty only once. Whilst I dealt with the Sergeant in charge and checked off items on the indent, Mick had a walk round to see what he could scrounge. He came back saying that there was rum and asked if we could have a ration as we had missed ours being away from the battalion. The Sergeant said he could not split a jar, but if he could find a half jar he would stretch regulations and let us have it. Mick came up with a sandbag with a jar in it and thanking the Sergeant was in a hurry to get back to the billet. He carried that jar carefully and finally placed it in the middle of the billet with much pride and exclamations of joy from his pals.

The day's duties over we congregated for the opening ceremony, everyone having either cup, basin or mess tin to partake of the 'dragon's blood'. The usual ration per man is measured in spoonfuls and to exceed that was dangerous but here was lashings of the stuff and we did not intend to reserve any as someone said:

"Why? We might all be casualties by morning." We were. The drinking began and tongues soon loosened until someone suggested we should see who could see the bottom of his cup first. Always the volunteer, with a "Here goes" I lifted my mug with a gill of rum in it and drank deep.

The effect was immediate; I nearly choked as I sat on the end of my bed. My last words were "Take his boots off" as they laid me on the bed. I do remember my last thoughts, which were:

"Cooky you've had your chips. You've heard of men dying from an overdose of rum, well it's your turn now" and then I lapsed into unconsciousness.

Next morning our little RAMC Corporal arrived to gather his workers but there was no response to his 'wakey, wakey'. We were all flat out. He went off to bring Sergeant Carlin. Now for trouble!

Carlin was a wonderful fellow but he could lash out with his tongue when he desired. He literally kicked us out of that billet, calling us a drunken lot of so-and-so's and never again would we go to the dump without an escort. Finally he chastised us severely for not telling him, nor inviting him and Punter to the swill, nor had we the decency to at least reserve a drink for their old campaigning pals. However we could take it as well as he could give it. The band as a body had been together too long and their spirits never fell. The sight of us was a picture and for myself, my main trouble was a head like a pudding and a mouth and throat like the sands of the desert. Darkie Matthews was the worst to look at. Darkie was a hardened drinker but this had really got him. I could just remember him sitting on an old kitchen chair with no back and his legs wrapped round the front legs of the chair. Quaffing his rum he roared with laughter and lifted his head back, only to lose control of himself and with a resounding bump hit his head on the hard floor, his legs still entangled in the chair.

Darkie was bald headed as long as I knew him and the lump in the back of his head the size of an egg was all the more pronounced and he could not wear his cap without a distinct forward tilt. Luckily we had no inspection to face on our parade as there was little sanitary work done that day. Later it was considered a great success and Mick and I were thanked for the party.

One thing it did for me, I never wanted rum again and I vowed that when I left the army I would become a teetotaller. I could excuse men in the infantry for drinking under the conditions we had in France but it was not for me.

CHAPTER EIGHTEEN

ARRAS

Easter Monday April 1917 saw the opening of the battle of Arras. Our little party was fortunate to be three miles away in Warlus but we were not unmindful of those who faced the cauldron of fire on that morning at dawn. The sky was lit up with a blood red glow as guns opened up simultaneously but to make matters worse the weather was atrocious with heavy sleet and bitter cold. Many hundreds of men must have died from exposure who otherwise would have been picked up eventually. I can only repeat what was told to me by those who were actually there on the spot and men whom I could trust.

Sitting in the assembly trench under the preliminary bombardment, waiting for the word 'go', is always an ordeal, as I know from experience. Most of these lads were very young and this was their first time in such a situation.

I do not doubt this story. A man was seen to leave the trench and run back away from the lines. He had not gone many yards before an enemy shell hit him and the explosion left nothing recognisable.

"Who was that?" someone shouted and a reply came:

"Sergeant..."

"Bloody good luck to him" several cried.

One does not like to think of such a thing happening and I never believed stories of disliked Officers and NCOs being shot in the back in actions such as this. I prefer to think it never happened. I've heard men say they would do it and I might have thought they had a good reason but always someone told them they wouldn't have the guts if the occasion presented itself.

In this case at Arras I found little sympathy for the man who ran away, not because he ran as many must have done, unable to stand the strain and shell shock. These young lads had been brought to France by that Sergeant from the depot and his reputation as a 'base Walla' was well known. I knew him and didn't like him at all. He had no intention of putting into practice the kind of bayonet fighting he taught at base, when he howled and drove almost frantic young men who were never intended to be soldiers. He liked nothing more than to take 'pack drill' for a squad of defaulters. It was a form of punishment cruel in the extreme and sometimes given for trivial offences. He always impressed his superiors by the efficiency and smartness of his platoon but his methods of getting such results marked him as the coward he became. My sympathies were with the lads who had to suffer him.

The story of the battle will be better told elsewhere but that opening day was a big reverse for the German forces, trapped in their deep dugouts, they surrendered 'en masse'. They were glad to reach the safety of our cages waiting for them after being pounded by the best gunners in the world, not to mention the infantry. They clinched the deal as always 'all for a shilling a day!'

It was on the 27th that we returned to the battalion with others including Officers, who had been in neighbouring villages. We counted ourselves very fortunate when we heard all that had transpired and saw the list of casualties. The regiment carries Arras amongst its battle honours and I like to think that in those early days of the battle those very young drafts and the older hands with them won the honour.

St George's Day had passed on the 23rd with the battalion at rest but we were sent the red roses, which we wore with pride in Warlus.

On the 29th we assembled again as a band and led the battalion to Church Service in an open field and our music was appreciated.

Again our work started in earnest for a soldiers duties are not with arms alone. Supplies must go forward and where transport cannot go, army boots can, so we picked up our loads night by night and trod the way regardless.

The next engagement in the battle was for us to take the village of Monchy held by the enemy just beyond rising ground east of Arras. Close to the famous Vimy Ridge. There was little instruction given as to how we were to gain possession. It was evident it had been tried before from the number of dead lying around, including cavalrymen with their horses who had been caught in barbed wire and cut off by the knees by machine gun fire. We advanced at night and it was extremely dark, our only light being the gun flashes and shell bursts. Singly or in twos and threes we reached the top of the rising ground only to be met with intensive gunfire from close range. My particular job was to carry large bundles of sandbags, feeling very vulnerable and helpless but knowing that the load was vital. Somehow we reached the front line, or rather where it was intended to be. It was merely marked by a number of men frantically digging in what looked like a tennis court, so little cover was there from the hail of fire. Here we learned the real use of entrenching tools that we had carried since first being kitted out but only used occasionally to chop wood or open a tin of bully beef. Like moles men dug in, some lying prone and keeping up a covering fire we were eventually below ground and from a mere funk hole were able to join a neighbour. Wonderful to relate by daylight we had a line of trench and hope for the day. However there was no communication trench so the way back for supplies and casualties was over open ground in full view of Jerry, who must have thought us sitting ducks. Situations like this bring out the best in men such as our battalions provided and here there was to be no going back. We had come and we would stay. We even dared to make tea in our mess tins over old letters and matchsticks.

Fortunately relief came soon and we left at night handing over a well-made foundation to what became a new front line for some time. Our casualties were heavy, officially reported as 36 killed, 133 wounded, 34 missing, yet after just one day's rest we were back again holding trenches to the east of Monchy for another week.

Here we saw the battle going on around us, our immediate duty to hold the trenches we occupied. They were lined with dead from previous fighting, mostly Scotsmen, kilts and all. We came in for a lot of shelling and had no rest being sentries all day and night.

One of our new Officers came alongside me at night as I pointed out the position of the enemy. After I had given him my report he said:

"What are we standing on?"

"Dead men Sir," I replied "Highlanders no doubt, they lie everywhere in this stretch of trenches."

"Good God, let me out of this place" he said as he left quickly for a safer spot, leaving me on my lonely vigil with a few dead bodies under foot. Yes, war is horrible and this is life at its grimmest, I thought. Here too no man's land was alive with crawling figures, revealed as Verey lights from both sides lit up the scene, figures in both grey and khaki but it was the grey we picked out as targets.

I seemed to get chosen as guide quite often, someone must have thought I had a flair for it.

Leading a company out for rest as far as Arras, I made my way back as guide to our own relief. I never knew what sense led me but I was never lost over ground littered with bodies. The flotsam and jetsam of an army guided me on, my landmarks a broken limber, some barbed wire or mere instinct, who knows? I remember Darkie Connor, probably a West Indian, and Johnny Corcoran, both Colonels' runners who carried messages through thick and thin, alone and seemingly regardless of shell and rifle fire and still arriving with a grin. Johnny came from Leeds and I met him years later working with navvies laying a tram track and a second time on Holbeck Moor one Saturday afternoon strolling along reading his 'Sporting Pink':

"Hello Johnny" I surprised him by interrupting his study of form for the day's racing.

"Hello Cooky" he replied with the same bright smile. I remember he said I looked prosperous and that he was glad to have any kind of a job in those grim days of unemployment. Perhaps to him I did but that may have been because I was with my girlfriend later to become a very loving wife. She remarked that I had some strange friends but I rebuked her as I told her I would never pass Johnny and his like unheeded.

I remember Darkie in Kemel days. We often met him as we made our way back and forth with stretchers. The regulars had a particular affection for him, as he had been their companion in India before the war. Neither of them is mentioned in the history of the battalion but their work meant success or failure in many instances.

My diary of the time tells me that on May 10th, after doing some fatigues, I was to guide a battalion coming out of the line. The following day I had to fall out of a Parade owing to sickness a most unusual thing for me. What it was I do not remember but if it was from bad smells I'd had a belly full!

Saturday the 12th, more fatigues at Tilloy and the weather had turned very warm. None of us were really fit so the camp at Simencourt and later Wanquentin housed weary men but there was no rest as parades kept us on the move, if cleaning up didn't. Yet we must have had some energy left as on the 16th we played a football match that I have reason to remember.

Wanquentin was a railhead where ammunition was unloaded and stacked in a huge dump and our football field was about half a mile away. During the match the ammunition dump went up in one terrific explosion taking away the village and all personnel on the dump. Bodies, shells, railway lines, everything went sky high and we had one man wounded on the field from falling debris. No one ever knew the cause but it was said that a German plane was seen just before the explosion flying very low. It was likely that he had dropped a bomb and if so he had scored a bull's eye. Life brightened again as we drew our instruments and formed up as a band with practices a welcome change before leading the battalion to billets at Manin where at last we rested comfortably.

A special engagement at the Officer's Mess became a talking point for many months amongst the bandsmen. It is questionable who enjoyed the evening most, the band or the Officers.

The occasion was the visit to the Mess by a former Officer of Indian days now known as Brigadier Platt. The only thing missing from his reception was the Regimental Silver (in safe keeping somewhere in Alnwick or Newcastle). Evidently as a young Officer he had been very popular as Dub, Smiler and all the old hands remembered him. In his honour we did an unusual clean up including buttons and brasses. 'Brasso' must have paid a dividend that year as we polished up and marched to our place of performance. We even had a second shave of the day and a close inspection by Sgt. Carlin. I was proud to accompany them though still the 'baby' in age and service.

The room we were to play in was adjoining the Mess proper and as I looked at my friends I remember thinking that 'All things bright and beautiful' would have been a good opening. They could have wished for no better star to the evening than when the Chief Steward asked us if we would have bottled Bass or a barrel with the compliments of the Officers. All immediately opted for the Bass. I noted some pleasant and surprised looks as they quietly placed the order, all in good taste as behoves gentlemen of the band.

"Forgot there was such a thing as Bass" Dub whispered to me.
The programme opened with a March 'Die Banda Compt' a snappy little German tune and we gave it full vent.

"The trombones are in good form tonight," said Punter approvingly at the end of this introduction.

"Thank you Bandmaster" I replied as it was the first time I had been complimented by him and no doubt the first time he had been addressed as 'Bandmaster'. He visibly swelled as he took up his baton again.

The beer had arrived as we played and in the centre of our circle stood a complete crate of bottled Bass, soon to be broached to whet the lips of all.

'The Overture to the Yeomen of the Guard' was the second item. The solo by Tommy on the euphonium was good, if rather pronounced in that little room, lit by numerous storm lanterns. Punter looked very pleased, as did others taking liquid refreshment in the intervals. The waiters had the good sense to shut the door between us and the dining room, as the voices were beginning to resemble a taproom in North Shields. 'La Paloma' was next with oboe and horn to the fore, Dub and Smiler also leading the field in disposing of Bass but still slightly behind Darkie Matthews on bass drum as he could drink whilst counting his bars rest, if not when he was actually on the beat.

He was the first to succumb as he leaned over his drum and did a complete somersault to the floor in front. We were supposed to be standing when playing but one or two had already taken seats on the crates and some stools.

Things got worse when we reached '1812' Overture. The gunfire from the drums was superb, played 'off the beat' as indicated and George Stoneham (side drum and effects) and Darkie, on his feet again, excelled themselves.

Finally Punter fell off his elevated perch and made no attempt to resume command. Heads nodded as they carried on, indicating to me to take the stand as I was nearest to him. It would have been disastrous if an Officer had looked in and seen our conductor 'hors de combat'. Fortunately I had not partaken, remembering the rum episode so I took the baton but with no idea where we had got to nor did I look very professional but I saw them through.

Somehow we managed to continue with some changes in the set programme and we heard clapping in the mess proper as we prepared for 'The King'. Probably they too had Bass mixed with stronger stuff! The hero of the performance was Harry Robinson, my Leeds pal. He played his baritone solo 'Simple Aveu' as never before, sweetly and smoothly although beer must have almost reached his ears! Harry was a Yorkshire miner and at one time a member of Rothwell Old Band so this was no new experience for him as it may have been to his army comrades.

We were told that Brigadier Platt had asked to speak to his old friends from the days in India before we left. Carlin took his place at the door leading to the exit to do the honours and introductions as we filed through.

"This is McQuade Sir. You will remember him in 'E' Company."

"Oh yes, I remember, Smiler wasn't it? How are you McQuade? So glad to see you again."

Nicholl, Matthews, Stoneham, Creighton, Corporal May and all were similarly greeted as hands were shaken with suitable replies in spite of the Bass. Robinson, myself and other war serving men were also introduced.

"And who is the man holding the lamp?" the Brigadier asked finally.

"Sutherland Sir, also of 'E' I believe and back from Reserve." Dub had been holding the lamp in the narrow passage lighting up faces to be recognised.

"Oh Sutherland" the General said "We knew him as Dub in those days. How are you old man?" as he stretched out his hand to Dub. Dub held his lamp, which was without glass, close to the Brigadiers face, almost singeing his smart military moustache.

"Hello Mr Platt, it's nice to see you again old man." He remarked in a very beery kind of voice, which sent shivers through Carlin, and some of us who were still there. Brigadiers of Mr Platt's calibre were not shaken by anything and he bid us goodnight as if nothing untoward had been said or done.

In high spirits we reached our billet, a barn with the usual threshing floor in the middle where we deposited our instruments with the big drum as the centrepiece.

Darkie complained next morning that his drumhead had got wet and was unfit for use until he had dried it tight so he must miss practice.

Punter wasn't pleased and told Darkie he was a fool to leave the drum in the middle of the floor. The mystery was solved and the Orderly man was blamed. He had failed to leave the urine tub last night! Someone said he thought he had heard thunder in the night!

Returning to Arras again, we split and rejoined our companies, to resume duties as riflemen and stretcher bearers, although the battalion had been brought up to full strength by new drafts. The weather deteriorated and the ground evacuated by the enemy was considerable. They had destroyed dugouts and trenches leaving us to rebuild or remake shelters and new trenches entirely. If Fritz had retired to what he thought a safer line, he certainly had a good supply of ammunition for his guns, which gave us no peace day or night. Their patrols stole up as close as they dare, keeping us on our toes.

I was asked again to take promotion, even directly to Sergeant but I refused. It was obvious that the NCOs who had brought the new drafts from England were pretty useless being conscripts themselves. No one had any confidence in them and I saw several instances where they funked on covering parties and in places of danger. The new Officers lacked experience and I was often sought for guidance on certain points of procedure of which they lacked knowledge. I was serving with 'Y' company and the Sergeant Major was CSM Taylor, a regular with a lot of experience, known to most of us as 'Tragedy'.

I never discovered the reason for the nickname but it seemed to fit him. He was every inch a soldier and whilst we younger men never used his nickname, he did not flinch when Smiler or any of the others referred to him as 'Tragedy'. It was fortunate that the company had him to smarten things up. There was no nonsense about Tragedy; he took his duties seriously, although at times he was a bit of a martinet. I shall never forget him as we buried a man who had been killed where it was essential to bury him behind the front line trench without the aid of a Chaplain.

The German trench was very close but it was very dark and quiet as we carefully placed the body in the grave we had dug under Tragedy's guidance. Then we stood round at attention whilst he made a smart unhurried salute to our fallen comrade. It was a silent service but one which impressed me and I saw my Sergeant Major in a new light. I thought of the lines I had learned at school:

"Not a drum was heard, not a funeral note:
As his corse to the ramparts we hurried...

We carved not a line and we raised not a stone:
But we left him alone with his glory"

About this time we had an amusing instance of the inexperience of a young Officer. Forming part of a large carrying party we set off in daylight on what we gathered was to be a long journey with rations in sandbags, two to a man, led by the Officer and a Sergeant. For hours we followed them. Darkness fell and still we travelled on, over the open, through innumerable trenches, the bags becoming heavier as we plodded on with much grumbling and remarks from companies we passed on the way. Struggling past one lot we heard:

"It's that bleeding party of Geordies again." Apparently we had doubled back on our tracks and tempers were not improved as someone remarked about.

"Silly bloody Officers who liked walking about in the moonlight."

Daylight broke and we were still on our way until finally we were allowed to rest in a sunken road with troops billeted in dugouts alongside; 'fed up and far from home'.

Our two leaders stood consulting a map with a very weary look on the Officer's face as he turned to us.

"Do any of you men know where the Brown Line is?" he asked.

"No" said someone "but I've got a brown pencil we can draw one."

The remark was ignored. We were lost, then one of the spectators of this caravan of rations, perplexed by our appearance from nowhere, said

"This is the Brown Line, Sir."

It was only left for us to locate the unit to be supplied and we turned back for home where the HQ must have given us up, if not already out in search of our bodies. Our rations might already have been distributed between the non-carriers we had left behind yesterday.

This platoon had very young lads, as green as they come, with the worst Sergeant of the lot. He was virtually useless but used his stripes for his own benefit and comfort. The lads were being cheated of any comforts, which occasionally came with rations. I noticed there was no milk at breakfast and asked them if they ever had any but they almost laughed at me for expecting milk in the front line trenches.

"There was milk in the bags I helped to carry last night." I said and went to the Sergeant's dugout to enquire. He was out and the dugout was empty except for some rations and six tins of Ideal Milk, which I took and walking along the trench distributed it, like manna from heaven, much to the delight of all.

Along came the Sergeant with threats of taking me to the Company Commander on a charge of stealing rations. I told him where to go but I would also bring a charge against him for the same thing but an 'old soldier' would bring his charge. Let him first make enquiries what that meant in this battalion. He did and I heard no more but noted that he lost his stripes a few days later. If he had asked Tragedy as he probably did, he would soon learn and he had probably already been marked for demotion.

I was becoming the oldest soldier in the Company – an ambition I had long desired for whatever people may say regarding the army pre-war and soldiers in particular, my opinion was that they had been sadly maligned as work shy and 'ne'er do good'. They had faults no doubt but put to the test as this war was doing, the 'old soldier' stood out alone. Never let us forget he not only held the line against tremendous odds in 1914 and early 1915 but he passed on his experience and training to thousands of men. He had no Trade Union; his pay was very poor especially for the infantryman and of all the services the infantry are indispensable even in these days of mechanised warfare. Imagine his feelings when he heard of strikes for higher pay in munitions factories or fortunes being made by those who escaped enlistment. We knew little of higher strategy, as we were never consulted.

Ours was a small world in a vast firmament of armies but what I saw and learned was seen by very few of those who visited France during hostilities and went home thinking they had seen it all. There was a vast difference between Army HQ, the supply lines down to the coast and the few wretched men who, isolated, wet and hungry, held a miserable depression in the ground with a very well trained enemy a stone's throw away. This we did at Hooge and other places. It was then that men were proved and the 'old soldier' was our rock, good as many of 'Kitchener's Army' became.

We had our saints too. For some weeks after Arras we engaged in an assortment of duties with only the occasional few days rest behind the lines. On one of those nights we sat in a meagre dugout awaiting instructions to go forward whilst the artillery prepared the way for us with a terrific barrage from both sides. A new man, named McAlpine had joined us. At one time he had been a candidate for the Church, was well spoken and not affected by the environment in which he now found himself. Quite the reverse, he wrote on the trench periscope "Watch and Pray." The duty Officer remarked to me:

"I know who had that periscope before you took over, McAlpine. He is a man in a thousand." I agreed.

As we, some six or seven men, sat in that little shelter waiting, he sat near the candle reading a Bible. He looked up and said:

"May I say something to you all?" We looked at him and he continued.

"You all know where we are going when we leave this place and in all probability someone will be killed if not badly wounded." We all listened intently, he was so earnest no one could fail to nor was there any joking.

He continued:

"Is there anyone here who is afraid to die?" What a question! After a short period of silence one man spoke.

"Yes Mac" he said "I am. You fellows seem to have no fears but I confess that I live in fear of being killed. I think of my wife and kiddies in York and feel as if I shall never see them again." The man's name was Cattle, born and bred in York, a very nice ordinary kind of man, quiet and likeable.

Mac talked to him, whilst others listened and tried to allay his fear by a faith which is above all faiths. He finished by asking me if I would, with him, help Cattle to gain confidence in himself and lose his fear of bullets 'with his name on' as we used to say. He suggested that when we went forward, Cattle kept close to us both and we would protect him and show him that the bullets he heard had already become the bullets that had missed.

This we did, as we advanced, took over an old German trench and established ourselves for a few days. I remember standing with Mac at night with head and shoulders exposed, persuading Cattle that there was nothing to fear. Gradually we got him up, full of nervous tension, to join us although it was risky to stay there longer than seconds as the whole place was raked by rifle and machine gun fire. I believe it worked though what happened to Cattle or Mac I never knew, for the battalion moved on and we resumed our old roles as stretcher-bearers, working from Head-quarter Company.

We had periods of rest when snug billets would have been very welcome but the enemy had devastated the whole country through which we passed. We were constantly moving so little could be expected and what comforts we had we made for ourselves from anything we could scrounge or improvise. The weather was very wet indeed and we seemed to be at the beck and call of Division to fill in gaps in the line and relieve regiments in need of rest. They needed it more than ourselves and we moved at very short notice to take up positions in a very thinly held line.

These were mere outposts, there being little in the way of a continuous line of trench. We were used for any kind of labour, even to building and repairing a light railway and transporting bricks and material from shattered villages.

At one camp in the region of Achiet-le-Petit, I was given the use of a mule and cart to transport bricks. This was new to me as I was anything but a horseman. Fortunately the mule was a quiet beast and we managed to live together quite amicably for a few days and built ourselves the most non-descriptive camp ever. With fittings salvaged from the village it seemed to be a competition with each other as to who could build the best 'villa'.

Town planning was unknown as we built to suit individual tastes, only when having made ourselves comfortable, to be told to pack up and hand it over to some new unit. It never seemed to be the other way about. Someone had the idea of producing a concert so talent was sought and a piano requisitioned. This was purely a battalion exercise. One reads of Concert Parties touring for the benefit of front line troops but so far we had seen nothing of these nor did we expect to. In our opinion they were like strawberry jam-only for those well back from the actual line. One of our 'wags' (and we had many) wrote a few lines to a catchy tune which expressed what I have just written.

"Please Mr Officer tell me do,
Do we get relieved tonight?
I've built a little sandbag trench and it really is all right,
Close very close to the sniper's post,
Where the aerial torpedoes visit us most,
If they come we will give them machine gun toast,
Way down whiz-bang lane."

Going on to say that he built for other's comfort, by some spiteful fate just waiting until he spread his blankets, before being told to move to pastures new.

It was surprising the talent we could produce and the humour still prevailing amongst men who had seen so much of the opposite.

Lt Colonel Herbert did more than any other had done in making life more bearable for men who seemed to get all the kicks and few of the halfpennies-the infantry, for surely we got a raw deal compared with others. If we wore our badges with pride they seemed to have little respect when it became our lot to spend a time at Base camp or in some better dressed units. They had the benefit of two suits and were able to keep clean in well-ordered camps and billets and got preference in service. There were times when we really felt like outcasts and bad feelings were engendered. No matter where we were and however many strangers we had to mix with, the Infantry badge brought us together again and many a friend was made by it. It was equal if not better than any Masonic handshake.

During this period when we had so many young lads with us, roughing it, as they never had before, this incident showed our Colonel's humanity and quality. The band was playing at his request to the men in the Village Square. When teatime approached the Orderly Men for the day were called to the Cookhouse. As they answered the call they saluted the Colonel who had been standing alone for some time listening to the band and surveying the scene. He was a good looking soldierly figure and immaculately dressed on this occasion. We had often seen him covered in mud and lacking a shave, for like us he was no stranger to the front line.

The bands-men stood relaxing between items in the programme as the Orderly Men came back carrying dixies of hot tea and food to their respective platoons. As they passed the CO they gave a smart 'eyes left' or 'right' their hands being fully occupied with their loads. The Colonel ordered one little group to halt and put the dixies down.

"What's in there?" he asked pointing to the large dixie.

"Tea, Sir" was the reply.

He asked for the lid to be lifted and a cup brought. One man dashed off to the nearest billet, returning with a pint pot, which he was wiping on his sleeve. Pint pots are scarce here and we wondered how he managed to have such an elegant drinking utensil. He handed it over with pride.

The CO dipped in for a sample of the brew, tasted as if it were wine at a party and threw the remainder of the pot into the gutter.

"Tip the whole lot out boys" he said "and tell the cooks to come here immediately. That's not tea, it's swill." Whilst the summons was being carried out, he enquired what was in the other receptacles.

"Bacon Sir" two or three voices replied at once.

"Bacon, you are lucky to have bacon for tea, aren't you? I thought bacon was for breakfast. Wouldn't you rather have it so or do you get it at both meals?"

He was told they got it for tea because the cooks say they haven't time to cook it at breakfast time. The Chefs arrived, both men well known to us all. They have had their jobs for a long time and had a reputation for stew, stew and more stew ever since the days at Ouerdam. Maybe the Colonel already had his suspicions. They were told in no uncertain terms what he thought of their tea and what he thought of these good young soldiers who needed better food than they were providing. The spectators and the band were able to hear every word as the climax was reached.

"You two " he said "do not go into the trenches, do you?"

"No Sir" they replied "but we see that the rations are supplied and we accompany the Transport to see they are delivered Sir"

They stood to attention, both men with some years of service, in their smoke grimed khaki with neckerchiefs tied round their necks.

"Go and make fresh tea for these men now, and in future you will get out of bed to cook bacon for breakfast, not teatime. In future you will take your place in a cookhouse as close to the trenches as possible, provide hot meals to the men in the line. I won't have this disgusting food for men under my command. Dismiss!" and with that they saluted, did a smart about-turn and left, no doubt feeling much smaller than their considerable physical stature.

So after three years of war, the effort was to be made to provide hot meals where they were really needed for the battalion. Others had already managed a better system than we had. We had seen men carrying containers of hot food strapped on their backs to the front line but no attempt had ever been made for our companies. As Stretcher-bearers, we had always been well looked after by George. No matter what the conditions, nor how dangerous, he always managed somehow to keep us well fed and faced the dangers himself of all-revealing smoke being seen by the enemy. When it came to washing up, George's dixies were spotless, the taste of stew ended when stew was finished and tea had to be made. I know of nothing nicer than George's toast, made on a heap of glowing embers of a wood fire but that is to speak of luxuries. To add to his accomplishments, George would take his place as a bearer when really necessary although he was he was not physically strong but he was also a useful third or fourth clarinet. His smiling face above a smoke grimed khaki tunic was a more pleasing picture than our company cooks.

When Smiler and I saved him at Longueval on the Somme we knew that life would never be the same again without him. His value was not just culinary, with his ready wit and good sense many an argument ended peaceably. If 'George said so' that was it, he had no enemies but lots of friends.

Periods of rest, with the inevitable fatigues and duties, did not take us away from the battle zone, which now extended deeply. Long range artillery with air reconnaissance, often made our camps a target for their activities. Air warfare was intensifying but anti-aircraft guns seemed to be as futile as ever with millions of shells bursting to no avail, except perhaps to hasten the flight of planes or confuse observers. We often watched the 'dog fights' with interest but their story is really no part of my narrative.

Our Colonel was one who could be numbered among the few casualties at this time, being slightly wounded as a shell passed between him and Harland and on bursting slightly wounded both.

A different tea story was told of two or three men who, during the advance on Arras. In the thick of things, they had dropped into a shell hole for cover and had the bright idea of 'drumming up' some tea before going on. They were discovered in the act by the Colonel himself who appeared at the edge of the hole with a fusillade of recriminations for men who thought of nothing else but tea when there was enemy to pursue. There were no faster feet in that advance than those erstwhile tea-makers as they abandoned their mess tins and flew in full flight Eastward, followed by their CO with revolver at the ready, as enthusiastic as if it was a football match. He and Captain Pease together made the battalion what it was and with fewer of the old trained soldiers, they prepared us for the battle that was to become the biggest 'blood-tub' ever. Captain Pease was to leave us before the opening of this battle, to transfer to the Royal Flying Corps after serving the battalion for nearly two years, the longest time anyone had held the post of Adjutant. He was a man greatly loved by all, particularly the men in the ranks, to whom a good Adjutant meant so much.

The intensive training, which now began, was something quite different from the normal routine exercises usually carried out by troops when withdrawn to rest. After the Divisional Commander gave a lecture to Officers of the 3rd Division explaining the tactics being taught, no doubts remained that there was to be a new offensive. In the ranks we never got the full text but it was perfectly obvious that we were working our way back to the Ypres Salient, which many of us knew so well. We knew that on June 3rd the British had finally taken Hill 60 and Messines

Ridge. Ypres was rumoured to be free of the threat of German invasion by the throwing back of the enemy to the S.E., East and N.E. of the town. We gathered too that the Brigade was to be in reserve for the first attack, to follow any success and carry the war into enemy territory, perhaps to end the war by Christmas.

The man power position must have been eased in spite of everything, for men were going on leave, such absntees not being missed except by their immediate friends. It was a welcome sign of things to come. My turn could not be far away, judging by several men who had already gone. The weather was still very wet and we had seen little of Summer sunshine and it was already approaching September. In fact by early September we were back in areas we knew as we read the signposts, Brandhoek, Zonnebeke, St Julien, all too familiar to those who had known the Ypres Salient earlier in 1915-16.

Eventually we reached Brandhoek by night, to take up billets in an area which was a congestion of units in a sea of mud, churned up by thousands of horses and their vehicles, plus lorries, guns and Caterpillar tractors trailing huge siege guns. The Labour Battalions too seemed to be in strength and seemed to be sharing the same piece of ground with them. The night of 22/23 Sept our battalion took over the line some-where in the vicinity of St Eloi, the Somme and Arras combined or so it seemed to me as I viewed it from the transport lines. I was told to report to the Orderly Room to collect my pass for leave to England. No one is left idle or at a loose end with the Fusiliers and I was Seconded to Transport until my departure-a job I had no inclination for at all but which I must face. Reporting to the Sergeant, whom I knew, I told him I was the world's worst horseman, knowing nothing about such beasts other than one end from the other. Sensing my fears, he promised me a quiet horse, in fact one almost blind but a good worker. Taking it to water meant riding bareback to the stream nearby, with only a neck chain to guide, but it followed its leaders placidly. All went well until it finally dropped its head to drink. How I failed to fall forward down that long mane into the deep, I cannot recall but we made it and eventually even managed to do a little grooming with a currycomb. My hands were shaking and I was afraid of being trodden underfoot whereas my fellow horsemen took as little notice of flying hooves as we did of spent bullets.

Rations and supplies were sent every night to the forward troops by pack-horse and following the first delivery to our men, after a difficult journey, they returned having lost two men and some horses, due to problems at Hell-fire corner. On the second night I was detailed to join in this run along with those who had rested the previous night, there being sufficient men to give one night on and one for rest, alternately.

Now I had been equipped with a new set of clothes ready for England with my pass in my pocket and the train ready to leave Ballieul at six in the morning. The Sergeant thought I should be excused, being so near a long awaited leave as the journey could be my last but I failed to see why I could not go and enquired what time we should return to camp. As this could be about 3am I said I would have ample time to catch my train. I had been up the line so many times under fire that I was beginning to think I had a charmed life. Finally he agreed but asked if I could do a favour for him.

"Cook, There is a new boy arriving today. He is a band-boy from Newcastle and I knew his Father who served with me in India." he said "Danny is a nice lad and you can show him the ropes and give him a few tips on his first time under fire."

So saying he brought Danny Pool to me, leading another packhorse and we took our places in the convoy now ready to move on. It was already dark and German planes were already dropping their loads on the many camps and supplies, the Labour Corps being badly hit.

Once through Ypres town, which was always running the gauntlet at night, we reached the beginning of the now famous 'Duck-board Track', the most dangerous trail to undertake. Single duckboards stretched for miles over a sea of liquid mud, a trap for the unwary be it horse or man. One walked along with eyes down , almost feeling the way with the reins behind one's back, hoping the animal would keep in line. One false step can mean drowning, as many must have done already and the battle is yet young. For me it was a quiet night, as I talked to Danny to my rear, explaining the meaning of star shells, like Joseph's coat of many colours, and telling him that the main bombardment did not seem to be in our direction. I hadn't a care in the world, with my pass in my pocket and hopes of seeing my loved ones soon, what was there to fear?

A call came from the rear to 'halt', a horse had lost its pack and we had to wait until it was secured before moving on. I had no idea where we were in the inky darkness, then out of the blue came the scream of a large shell, which dropped only yards away and exploded. Confusion ensued as horses scattered; men shouted instructions and tried to regain some order. I felt a blow like being burned by a red-hot iron in my arm and leg but held the horse, which never flinched.

"I'm hit" I called to someone who took the horse's reins and told me to get back down the duckboards as fast as I could before the next one dropped. As far as I know there was no second shell but I moved quickly. The duckboards disappeared and I found myself hopelessly lost in moments and was apparently alone. I heard someone calling and made my way to a shell hole only to find Captain Evans the Transport Officer lying there badly wounded. By now I realised I was in the same state with little chance of getting him away or attending to his injuries whatever they were. It seemed to me he was in a serious condition, surely there must be men close by who could help if I could find them. Telling Evans I was myself wounded but would bring him help quickly, I made my way by some instinct, finally shouting for help as loud as I could. West Yorkshire stretcher-bearers who called and guided me to them answered my calls. They immediately tore my trouser leg and revealed my injury in the left buttock, bleeding profusely. I told them to first let me take them to Captain Evans so we went and found him again.

By good fortune we were very close to our battalion HQ in a large German pillbox dressing station and all complete, where I was attended to, being placed on a stretcher to await being moved back to base.

Captain Evans was brought in by the West Yorks on a stretcher and immediately handed to the doctor within two or three feet of me. It was obvious that his injuries left little hope of his surviving but he told the doctor what had happened. He was badly hit and his horse bolted throwing him into a shell hole. Had it not been for one of his men who was also wounded he would have died out there but this fellow unable to do anything else brought assistance as he had promised.

His last wishes were that his wife should not be informed for another month as she was expecting her first baby and the doctor promised to see to that. He also asked the doctor to find out who the man was who helped, "One of my own men" he said and he should be mentioned in despatches but that was no help to me. Now my leave was definitely off and what would the Sergeant say when I didn't return. At my request an orderly went to the door of the bunker where some men were talking, to see if they could by any chance be Northumberland Fusiliers.

"Hello Cooky, what are you doing here? We all thought you had gone on leave." It was Harry Robinson, my Rothwell friend called to my side He said he would tell the others who would be sorry but hoped I would get a longer leave at least now that I'd got a 'Blighty One'! Harry was experienced at recognising a 'Blighty' from a scratch so my hopes lifted.

The night passed as the casualties kept coming in, the pillbox evidently being a target for the enemy guns which were so well calibrated that we had a direct hit on top. The concrete was so thick that although the place shuddered we suffered no harm.

Footnote

Years later I visited Tyne Cot Cemetery on the Passchendaele Ridge, Ypres with my son, there to see this very pillbox now partly sunk in the earth by sheer weight. It is surrounded by a vast array of neat graves of my unfortunate comrades, now lying at peace in a very well kept garden of rest. It is the biggest cemetery in the Salient and takes its name from the Regiment's base and as a place of pilgrimage is well worth a visit.

CHAPTER NINETEEN

WOUNDED

Now I was on the same journey that I had sent many others on, in the care of the RAMC, who took me to the Casualty Clearing Station near the town of Ypres. They remarked on my clean underwear and Khaki and I told them I was dressed for leave and had my pass and travelling warrant in my pocket. They consoled me with the news that the warrant would not be needed and that my leave was assured but not just yet. The Casualty Clearing Station was in the open with a number of both walking and carried wounded and many cases of gas poisoning. There was no confusion only steady preparation to get men away to safer surroundings as soon as possible.

Constantly under fire, the ambulances made their way to the nearest railway there to take the hospital train where we were given all the care those wonderful nurses could give us. For the time, rank is forgotten, the need is all that matters. Our immediate destination is Rouen so it was back to where I started in June 1915.

I took my place in the queue and was eventually lifted on to one of many operating tables in a large theatre. I saw little but the faces around me as I was immersed in a brilliant light. As I drifted into oblivion I just remember a nurse making some remark that I had not had this portion of my anatomy washed for me for a long time. Hours later I came to; lying on a floor lined with stretcher cases, many vomiting from the fumes of the ether. Fortunately it did not affect me. I drank some water and settled down to await the next stage, covered with a grey blanket, which on inspection I found to be alive with lice. I threw it off hoping none had penetrated to my newly washed body. I made no complaint in case it should delay my departure, for I saw we were very near another hospital train that was to take us to the docks. We were sent to another hospital there where we spent some days waiting for a suitable time in the moon's phases to cross the Channel. We were told a Harvest Moon makes hospital ships a target for enemy submarines. I lay comfortably in a clean bed in an immaculate ward but on looking down at my clean white sling holding my damaged arm I saw the biggest 'chat' ever to grace my person. I feared that he might not be alone and I should suffer the indignity of being 'deloused', which I have heard is quite an ordeal involving carbolic baths. I crushed the offending monster and prayed for cleanliness. All was well and it was the last for a long time.

The trip home on the good ship 'Warilda' was finally over and the sun shone on the white cliffs of Dover but we disembarked at South-ampton, where the quayside was completely covered with stretcher cases. Willing and loving hands came amongst us with comforts and offers of posting cards to family and friends to tell of our arrival. The sound of an English boy's voice brought tears to my eyes. I had forgotten such a sweet sound as I had lived with adults for so long. I lay there thinking 'Home at last'!

However I had a lot to learn. So far all had gone well since leaving the line. Our welcome and treatment had been superb but Army disci-pline penetrates even to its hospitals, as we were to find. Our ultimate destination was Stourbridge, to be inmates of a former workhouse, now a military hospital. On first sight it looked grim and the staff seemed to take a delight in making life uncomfortable. The food lacked taste and visitors and officials seemed to give me a wide berth until I began to wonder if I was infectious. One day a fellow patient said:

"You don't seem to attract many visitors, Fusilier. Have you any idea why?"

"No but I'd like to know" I said.

"On these beds there are little bows of ribbon indicating religion. I think so far your particular Padre hasn't been in, but what keeps the others away is that there is also a notice on your bed you cannot see."

"What does it say?" I asked.

"IMBECILE" was the reply, "and as none of us can yet walk about we couldn't remove it for you. The staff seem to think it proper to wait until higher authority gives the order."

Sister gave no apology when I asked for its removal. She seemed to take a violent dislike to my neighbour, a Scotsman with a very severe stomach wound. He was the most helpless man in the ward and one to whom morning porridge was an offence, far removed from that which his countrymen lived on. His complaint brought him into disgrace. He was reported to the Medical Officer and reprimanded for being insubordinate to Sister.

"I'm sorry laddie," he said "I have no alternative but mark you 'out'. She has the last word in such cases."

This was grossly unfair and the subsequent row between Jock and the Sister showed her to be a real 'Battleaxe'. Her fury turned on me and I too was marked 'out' but our means of going was an added punishment. Neither Jock nor I had put our feet to the ground since leaving the front line, he being much worse with stitching right across his abdomen preventing him standing upright but 'out' we had to go.

With kitbags full of new equipment and clothing, we left in an ambulance as sitting cases to Birmingham station, there to change and make our own way to a train some platforms away. Jock was incapable of carrying his bag but the ambulance dumped us and left us to manage.

Taking his bag as well as my own we proceeded slowly on our way until a gentleman asked us where we were going.

"Evesham" I said "If we can ever reach the train." He immediately took us in hand, summoned a porter and led us to the train, seeing us comfortably settled. He told us what he thought of people who could leave us in such a state. So we left what was to me an eye-opener on Military Hospitals. Fortunately it may have been an isolated incident but like Jock 'I had me doots'.

Evesham proved to be quite the opposite. We were met by ambulance and taken to what had been a private house and estate in lovely grounds, Abbey Manor. It was now a convalescent hospital run by civilian staff and some of the owner's retainers were still in service for our benefit.

Jock was soon in bed receiving every attention and likely to be for a long time. The food was first class, cooked in an immaculate kitchen by the best of female cooks. After a few days I no longer had to be confined to bed and was soon able to take a walk with others in the surrounding area. Evesham at that time was a delightful small town with people who showed us every consideration and hospitality.

After fourteen days of luxury I was pronounced ready for 10 days leave, twice the length of time I was originally due. My eldest brother Jack of the York and Lancs was also home having been gassed but returned to France after some weeks perfectly fit. The news of my crossing the Channel had been followed the next day by news of his homecoming. It was very welcome news for anxious parents who, like others, lived in daily fear of War Office Telegrams. We had a happy holiday in Leeds in spite of rationing and restrictions. Life went on much as before but I noticed again the indifference of some that were not involved but sought the rewards of a full labour market and easy profits. When will men learn not to make profit out of war but as I write, I recall the same thing in the next war to follow.

My leave finished and I reported to Ripon there to convalesce in a well-run camp at Studley Royal. Although this was back to the army, we had a good reception, met at the station by a considerate Sergeant who conducted us to the Camp at a more leisurely pace. All looked bright and beautiful after some camps we had seen. Yes! This is the army at its best, showing that it can do things well when it tries.

The hut to which I was allocated had six or seven Fusiliers from its fifty-two battalions and we soon became pals. The other thirty men came from the Midlands.

Why do all comedians come from Tyneside, Yorkshire, Lancashire and London, not forgetting Will Fyfe and Harry Lauder from Scotland? Have they any funny men in the Midlands? The bunch we had here must have been poor representatives of their native counties. They never joked between themselves, nor did they laugh with us and our humour fell on deaf ears or dulled minds. What they did attempt in the way of fun seemed childish and I cannot bring to mind one comedian of note from there.

On pay night they went together to Ripon, whilst we stayed in camp and enjoyed an excellent canteen then sat round a warm stove playing cards and having a sing song amongst ourselves. After all we were convalescents and after being in France appreciated this comfort and relaxation. We noticed that they were mostly on home service or if they had been abroad had probably not heard a rifle fired in anger.

The party of revellers returned just before 'lights out' when we were already in bed. They made a lot of noise evidently having drunk too much Yorkshire Ale. A Corporal from our 9th Battalion, wearing the Military

Medal was in charge of our hut and like the rest of us was recovering from wounds. He was a quiet, very likeable Geordie, not tall but powerfully built.

The revellers made for his bed, evidently a pre-planned scheme, with remarks not usually made to a full Corporal. He sat up in his trestle bed.

"I give you one minute to get to your beds. If you don't I'm going to put you there." We could see this was his last word and sensed what was to follow. The Staffs made no move but added, "Try it on."

There was a pause and tension like that in a Western film just before the hero draws his gun and the barman lowers himself behind the counter, then the explosion! With one leap Geordie was out of his bed. His fists flew like windmills as first one and then another dropped between their blows. Bedboards lifted, trestles scattered as we curled up out of harms way. Our help was not needed.

Finally we were down in bed and lights went out. The only sound was an occasional moan. The sick parade next morning saw a number of Midlanders limping with sprained ankles, black eyes, dislocated jaws and so on. Our champion made no reference to the affray and bore no scars but we noticed a quiet respect for his orders as NCO in charge of the hut and inspection parades.

'The Fighting Fifth' had won another battle single-handed.

One more incident I remember at Ripon camp. In the afternoon we usually spent a quiet time round the fire talking or just resting, as all good soldiers know how. The door opened and in walked the strangest man we had ever seen. Had he been a mere tramp we would have been less surprised. He was dressed in khaki which must have seen a rag store, buttons if not missing were replaced by civilian bone buttons, no puttees, civvy shoes more fitted for a dance floor than a parade ground and topped with an old cap which held the badge of the Fifth Fusiliers.

He quietly threw down a kit bag, which gave a metallic rattle from its one article of kit, a brass button stick, and joined us at the fire. With a "What Cheor!" he was recognised as a son of the Tyne and we made him welcome. Someone handed him a fag, another produced some tea and we made room for him on the form we sat on. His tongue loosened by the preliminaries we heard his story.

He returned from Salonika with our 2nd Battalion and on the troop ship was on a full dress parade for inspection. Checked for some misdemeanour he got involved in an argument with his Sergeant, which ended by him placing his thumbs beneath his shoulder straps. Having already loosened his belt, he lifted the lot including his rifle and calmly dropped the lot into the blue Mediterranean Sea, with the remark in loud and broad Geordie:

"Sergeant. I'll soldier nee mair" and he meant it.

To prove his story he proudly presented his Pay Book with the entry.

Debit- To one full infantry kit with rifle...£120-0-0.

To be deducted from pay.

On leaving hospital whilst on leave he had sold his newly issued kit, replacing it from goodness knows where and spent the lot. He had a kit-bag, why we did not know, as it only contained a button stick and the bag looked as if it had been used by a rag and bone man, which was quite likely.

He got a new kit and we fitted him up with smalls from our surplus until payday arrives. He paraded with us as we assembled at the Quartermaster's Office prepared with a trestle table covered with a brown blanket. A very young 2nd Lieutenant was in attendance, probably doing his first pay parade, the QM with his Pay Sheets and the Provost Sergeant to see we did not steal the cash.

As a name is called out, a man marches smartly up to the table, salutes and takes his pay, (five shillings for me) accepted as an honorarium. Our new friend waited for no name; he watched his chance and marched in a very soldierly manner, saluted and gave his name and number. The quartermaster looked at his sheets carefully running his finger down the columns.

"Your name is not entered here. Give me your Pay Book" he said.

"I haven't got one Sir"

"Where is it? You must have had one when you came here."

"No Sir. I've never had one since I left Salonika Sir, and they told me when I last enquired for one that you would give me a new one Sir."

There was a whispered conversation between the two financiers, which ended with the senior rank saying:

"We don't believe your story. You must have had a Pay Book and you may have lost it. We will write to records for your account. Meanwhile I will let you have five shillings which can be deducted from your pay when the book arrives and we get things straightened out."

What Records had to say we would have liked to know? The five bob would most likely be a loss to a very young Officer who will know better next time.

The Northumberland Fusiliers have some very cunning soldiers!

CHAPTER TWENTY

EAST BOLDON

After being passed A.1, a party of Fusiliers were sent by train to East Boldon, near Sunderland. I had heard of this place from several others and it had gained a reputation for itself before we arrived. It was the Depot of the Regiment for war-time only and was a model of neat huts aligned by a very taught string, as was everything else, including fire buckets outside the Guard House, where an immaculate sentry performed his duties as befits the famous Fifth.

It all started as we alighted at a small railway station.

"Fall in here" a loud voice cried, "You're in the army now. Come out of that tea room and get fell in. What do you think this is, a Sunday school outing?"

This came from a resplendent figure with buttons shining like stars and the peak of his cap almost touching his nose, thus keeping his head up at all times. We noted his arm-band, RP. This was no Cassidy Cannon of Poperinghe fame but this man had no kind instructions as how to walk about in a smart and soldierly manner. He strutted as to the manner born and we were supposed to wilt but he didn't know us yet nor has he recognised our Salonika pal.

We marched through the village with no greeting from the populace as they are used to 'rookies' here. We were given a meal in a large dining hut smelling of carbolic soap, and then we were allotted to platoons in separate huts. We marched in to the sounds of heavy boots on floor-boards until we got the order to 'Halt'. Our new Sergeant took over and in this narrative we will call him 'Samson' in case his corpse rises to castigate me for what I am going to say about him. My neighbour whis-pered to me:

"A hard –bitten b....r this", which brought an immediate

"No talking in the ranks. You are not in France now. This is where you learn to be soldiers. I will have no more of it."

So now we know! These are soldiers; we are mugs or ex-cannon fodder. Checked for name and number we were allotted beds noting the precision of the layout and the shine on the central pot-bellied stove where even the larger lumps of coal were whitewashed. Surely no one had ever spit on that stove to hear the hiss of its conversion to steam or the rebuke from one's opposite number who gets the residue in the eye, No fun here!

We gathered around the stove when his eminence had gone to his little bunk in a corner by the door, out of sight. His previous employ-ment during his days on army reserve had been in the employment of the Home Office as a prison warder, hence his mouth like a rattrap and his black moustache accentuating its bite. It was soon apparent that two insignificant individuals sitting near the stove were his cronies and we labelled them 'batmen'. In addition to doing his daily washing they kept him informed of what was said in his absence. I said to my pals:

"They must have thought we came out with the onion boat. It sticks out a mile what they are."

At Reveille we were all up and hurrying to dress for parade and to be first at the ablutions at the end of the hut. There were ten shining brass taps and on a shelf above ten glittering wash bowls. I selected one, only to be told that it is not for use and I must use the one everyone else was using; an old battered object covered in scum. I continued to use my clean bowl. No sooner had I finished than Samson came roaring in at me:

"You'll follow the rules here my lad or your feet won't touch. Use that bowl again and you're in clink. Get a move on and outside on parade."

We fell in outside the hut, Samson inspected us with his gimlet eyes, followed by an Officer who so far had only been wounded at Arras and had come here to learn how to be a soldier. He did not speak and I thought of Matthew 5 verse 5 'Pity the meek...' Poor lad he hasn't the backing I have in the ranks.

Marching off to a 'left, right, left' we reached the parade ground for the CO's inspection. He came round with his second-in-command, a man whose aim in life seemed to be to make other people miserable. Rifles here were for show and to make a noise without using ammunition. The crack as we slapped them to slope arms could be heard in Jericho, but be one second out of time and one's head was almost displaced with a roar of abuse. I only once heard Samson crack a joke. A man dropped his rifle on parade.

"Save the bits. We'll make a button stick out of them." It was not original; I had heard it many times before.

Several of us decided we would soldier here no more than we were forced and if Samson wanted trouble he could find it. We would dodge everything we could, keeping ourselves in the clear. This was not easy, as every member of staff seemed to be in league. Their one dislike was men from France.

Sergeant Major Drayson greeted me between parades, he too being a passenger after hospital treatment. He showed his delight in meeting one of his old platoons and was surprised to see me without at least a Sergeant's stripes.

"Had you taken them when we offered them to you. Cook, you'd have been a Sergeant Major by now."

Yes I might, with a wooden cross over my head was one thought, but the main one was that I was happy as I was, even here. No Sergeant's Mess for me, I liked the lad's company where I was. I would rather 'muck-in' and take life as it came. He told me that he would be glad to leave here. There was no place for him as for us. He had too much experience and placed their cushy jobs in jeopardy.

These incidents are no exaggeration. Rifle inspection by the Armourer was always strict but we were warned that this fellow here was mustard and had only one eye. Samson did his own inspection first but I thought if I couldn't clean a rifle by now I never would and I had no fears.

Parading outside, Armourer 'Nelson' came along the lines taking each rifle into his own hands removing the bolt and holding it skywards to inspect it. With mine he definitely used his blind eye, I had witnesses to confirm it.

"Take his name" he said to Samson and I was duly recorded 21235 Pte. Cook.

The two Officers following the Armourer heard this and also examined the rifle, one saying to the other:

"A bit keen, isn't he?" They asked me if I had cleaned it before parade.

"Yes" I told them "and the Sergeant passed it."

The same evening we were sitting round the stove and every few minutes a name would be called out and someone went into Samson's cubicle. Finally it was my turn. Shutting the cubicle, door Samson sat on the bed with his notebook in his hands.

"You were checked this morning for a dirty rifle. Was it dirty?" he asked.

"You inspected it before I went on parade" I said "and you know very well that rifle was perfectly clean. That's one thing you can't teach me, how to clean a rifle." It was a bit saucy but he seemed to be in a good mood and relaxed. He told me that he could not countermand the Armourer's word but he did not like men being on a charge, especially regarding rifles. I asked him what his duty was in the circumstances and was told that he would have to bring me up before the Company Commander in the morning and charge me and that offence would be put against my records to my detriment in the future.

"Sergeant" I replied "You talk of duty often and as a good soldier I think you ought to do your duty now. As to records I have no interest in them at all and if I get 14 days CB what do I care? I shall be leaving here for France before then I hope and it will be cancelled. Sergeant do your duty, I'll see you in the morning."

So saying that I left and rejoined my friends round the stove. I had a tip-off from a friend who had been in just before me that for a shilling Samson would cancel the record. He had paid his bob and recommended me to do the same as others did. This I told my friends and the little company round the stove, including the two stool pigeons. I added that if I was charged in the morning, which I hoped I would be, I would 'blow the gaff' to the presiding Officer and ask for the two Officers from the parade and the men who had already paid their shillings to testify.

Quietly one 'pigeon' slid off his seat and strolled nonchalantly to the cubicle, no doubt to report. I was never charged with having a dirty rifle, apart from by a one-eyed RAOC man and his words were wasted.

If only he had carried out his threat to charge me I would have raised such a stink in that camp as never was. It was corrupt to the core.

Now I was indeed a marked man with every staff instructor's hand against me but little did I care. I got 14 days C.B. for being absent three days after leave but never did one fatigue, nor missed a night out in Sunderland with my pals. I usually volunteered for cookhouse defaulters. On entering one is given two greasy dixies and told to collect ashes from the stoves and go outside and clean the dixies until they shine. I collected the dixies and the ashes and left them outside, moving off with a pal out of sight.

NCOs who were from active service, like us often handled defaulters. The staff were making merry in the Mess.

"21235 Cook" the Sergeant called checking the roll of delinquents.

"Hello Cook I didn't know you were here, fall out lad, and go and enjoy yourself."

It was Sergeant Newsome doing the work of Orderly Sergeant temporarily, in the evenings only, when the Higher Command 'Baccy' and his like have no interest in the super-efficiency of their regular staff working to save their home jobs. They had not had the experience of more seasoned men.

My fourteen days to barracks was imposed on some 83 of us who having been given ten days leave were due back on Friday. It was decided this was not good enough and that we would all return on the Monday. The authorities would have to decide what to do with 83 men absent from duty after ten days leave. There were no defaulters amongst the conspirators. I arrived by train at Newcastle to change for Boldon on Monday. Strolling along the platform awaiting the Boldon train I was accosted by two Military Policemen.

"Got a warrant soldier?" they asked. I produced it and handed it over. "You are overdue."

"Yes I know that, but I'm on my way back now." For the first time in my life I was arrested. (When I visit Newcastle now, I always walk to the very spot, prompted by nostalgia). The guardroom was the Waiting Room where quite a crowd of my friends was already gathered as we waited for the rest. The Redcaps saw us on to the train and we were on our way to Boldon where the reception party would be waiting. There we were marched under escort to the camp. We were in high glee as we thought 83 men would take some accommodating in the guardroom but instead we were told to rejoin our platoons.

Next morning a Regimental Police Sergeant took us to stand trial by 'Baccy Jack'. We went in singly as our names were called, to taste the discipline of Boldon's Military Court of Justice. On entering to a loud 'Quick march, left, right, left' one's cap was swept off his head so saluting was excused. This indignity was so that a man could not throw his cap at the Judge, nor could he kick the table up with his foot as an MP stood behind him watching his feet just in case. In spite of this it had often been done here, to the confusion of the court and added punishment to the offender, who later became a hero to his pals.

Meanwhile I was awaiting my call with an anxious Corporal who was concerned at the length of my hair.

"You'll get me hung. How did you dodge the barber?" he asked.

I knew he was taking men to him before the parade so I found it convenient to attend to a call of nature just then. He took my cap off, spit on his hands and plastered my hair down as well as he could. The list of prisoners for trial was not in alphabetical order and I found I was the last man. Having gone through the indignity of the 'cap-off' exercise Baccy heard my charge:

"When on Active Service three days absent from duty"

"Anything to say?" he asked me.

"Only that I took the extra three days as my Father was ill, Sir, and this is my last leave before joining the draft for France." (True in part only).

Telling me that had I asked for compassionate leave it might have been granted:

"Fourteen days to barracks. About turn, quick march" and I was on my way out, picking up my cap and finally being told to "Get your hair cut!" He had noticed in spite of my hairdresser.

To say "Three days pay and fourteen days confined to barracks" eighty three times in one hour was too much for Baccy so when our names and sentences were read out I noted that mine ends with only fourteen days to barracks. Had he been tongue-tied and forgotten the pay or had my appeal born fruit? I'll never know. However I was immediately marched under escort to the barber's shop to have a 'jailbird' crop, being left with only a little fringe above my eyebrows according to King's Regulations.

It fell to my lot to be on Headquarters Guard, a twenty four-hour duty beginning at sunset being called by bugle. This was a smart guard equal to anything at Buckingham Palace, except for the scarlet and the setting. We were given the day to clean up the equipment etc. and excused other parades. Most men spent every minute polishing buckles, buttons, and boots, even to the soles and insteps being dubbined. Khaki straps and haversack were slung in the hut to dry after a liberal application of blanco and so on, ad lib. As for my pal and me, we made our way by a known exit in a hedge for the day in Sunderland, returning for tea. We had numerous warnings offered as to what would happen when we went out for inspection but with little time left we did a clean up. Brasses were easy but webbing had a good dry clean with a hard nail brush only.

Samson was furious as he looked to two 'scruffy' soldiers he had picked for duty himself, no doubt fearing the consequences. Time was too short and he had no redress so we finally mounted guard after Baccy's ceremonial inspection. This was usually done to an audience of those interested in ceremonial drill and young Officers learning the ropes.

We felt like two ugly ducklings amongst swans but it must have been our 'soldierly bearing' which saw us through. We were both First Battalion men and who could equal them at fixing bayonets and presenting arms. It was child's play to us and our egotism increased as the ceremony proceeded. Finally it was all over, sentries posted, their duties read aloud from the typed board always hanging in the sentry box. Those not due for immediate sentry duty, including myself, departed for the guardroom to relax.

There were two guardrooms at Boldon, each a large hut and always full of the worst characters in the camp. Strong barbed wire and a padlocked door separated them from us. Like raging lions they greeted the new guard by clamouring at the wire, intent on lynching us it seemed. The main object was to see who was the Sergeant of the Guard and seeing Buck Adams (mentioned earlier) I feared the worst and Buck blanched. Some had old scores to settle and said so; others just had a grievance with everything military.

When the time came for them to visit the latrines we escorted them with fixed bayonets. There was no trouble until it came to the leader, a mountain of a man, who I confess scared others and me. Buck said he should go by himself with two guards and the instructions were to be very wary of his making a dash for freedom. To make matters worse Buck wanted to handcuff him but the handcuffs would not fit those wrists, which were like hams.

He raved about being sent alone when others went in twos but finally conceded the point as we escorted him outside. There he quietly turned to me and said quite calmly:

"Don't worry lad, I'm not going to cause any trouble for you. It's that little b****r I'll get some day." We did not repeat this to Buck as we padlocked him King Kong back amongst his friends for the night. Nevertheless we lost three men, who during a rough game amongst themselves, removed some of the boarding and slipped out in the dark.

If there were some potential criminals there, most of them were quite good soldiers. Only the silly rigid discipline in the camp and its very bad man-management held the blame for their unruly conduct and a little of the milk of human kindness would have removed the greater part of it.

To break their high spirits there was the added punishment of pack drill, usually held in the evening when a squad of men under the Regimental Police would do a full hour of intensive drill, with never a moment to stand at ease. Equipped with a full pack weighing 6olbs, plus rifle and bayonet, they were kept constantly on the move, finally being dismissed to double back to barracks wet with sweat and almost beaten into the ground. There were few spectators except for Baccy Jack who would be there to see that there was no slacking. If he got any satisfaction out of it did he ever consider the hatred he bred, not only to himself but also to his staff? If ever by some mysterious chance Samson should ever read this (I hope he doesn't) let him consider how he treated Private Bentley.

I first met Bentley at Ripon. Like myself he had been in hospital, badly wounded and had the misfortune to be at Boldon. Perhaps he would say good fortune, for several of us helped him out whilst he was there. He had been a farmer's boy before the war, he looked it, he talked like one, and it was ingrained in him. He had a very kind nature, he laughed at our jokes and leg pulling, which was perhaps new to him, as there were few jokes on the lonely Northumberland farm where he was brought up. In all, he was a very nice fellow but never cut out to be a soldier on a parade ground but was doing his best. If he had one outstanding feature it was his head, a size too big for his body and fitted with a cap two or three sizes too small. I take size 7, but it was like a pea on a drum on his head. Samson never let him forget this, from the first day he was told to 'Put your cap on straight' and repeated on every parade he ever did at that camp. It became not only embarrassing to him but an annoyance to us. If Samson had any sense he would have got him a new cap from the Quarter-master's stores, instead of trying with his own hands to make a quart go into a pint pot.

To add to his troubles, on his re-fitting after hospital, someone had cheated him out of some of his small kit, a hairbrush in particular, which we supplied to him from our surplus. Kit inspection at Boldon was an imposition for any man. All kits were laid out in line with string and in strict order. Woe betides anyone who lacked anything down to a piece of darning wool. Samson made more fuss about that missing hairbrush than if it had been the crown jewels, stamping and raging until the rafters shook with poor Bentley standing there almost in tears. Why we never mutinied there and then is one of the wonders of the war, but there was no spare brush anywhere.   After inspection by the Orderly Officer of the day, Samson had already taken his name as we cleared the kit away.

"Cooky" he said, "Next time I go to Sunderland, should I buy a brush?"

This he did out of his miserable pittance of sixpence a day but he never got a new cap whilst I knew him. He was glad to return to the steel helmet that must have been made for giants and few men ever got one that fitted.

At last our day of release came and the draft marched away to the station led by the band to the tune of 'Tipperary'. Few of us had any sweet girls to leave behind at Boldon and the inhabitants had become so used to seeing drafts going away that it seemed commonplace and of little significance to them.

We were proud to belong to the 'Fighting Fifth' but Boldon did them no credit. Their training had little to do with the soldiering we had to do again once we left these shores. I looked back to the days at Whitley Bay when Colonel Friend, Sgt-Major Bill Hodgson and Sgt. Pearson ran a camp as it should be run and they never needed two guard rooms like those at Boldon.

Now I could see why those young soldiers at Arras had wished their Sergeant 'good luck' as he was blasted into eternity as he was deserting under fire. He had been one of the staff at Boldon and had a reputation as bad as Samson's, but not having the physique of the ex-warder, used more subtle methods to make himself very unpopular. It is a sad thought that whilst in war so many gallant deeds are done and so much good comradeship engendered between men of all classes, that there are still those who take a delight in making another man's life a misery. Men like Smiler McQuade, Dub Sutherland, Syd Jowett and many more I know, stand out like stars in the firmament; they had no mean streak in them. These are the men I remember and who knows, most likely it is such a man who lies in Westminster Abbey, 'unknown' except to his God. They lie in their thousands in France and in these affluent days, so few of those hurrying South on holiday have a few minutes to spare to visit their earthly resting place. They are 'Known Unto God', if it were not so then surely all they did was in vain.

To the strains of the Regimental March, the train eventually moved away but it could not drown the catcalls of abuse hurled at our late tormentors. The bad boys from the guard room were three men short when we reached Folkestone, having slipped away at York when we stopped for a quick snack provided from a trolley on the platform. We wished them well!

CHAPTER TWENTY ONE

BACK TO FRANCE

After leaving Dover we crossed the Channel and arrived at the base camp at Etaples. It was now March 1918 and the enemy was known to have gained the advantage of troops from the Russian front to concentrate on the offensive in France. Our arrival coincided with the opening of this momentous event. The battle was already in progress having opened on the 21st of the month, the first day of spring and as too often when the Germans opened a move, the weather favoured them. For our forces the reverse seemed to happen, this was a glorious spring. News reached us of fierce fighting and German advance hotly contested by our armies who were holding out where they could. When we saw for ourselves the message to all troops posted up at headquarters from Field Marshall Haig that we had 'our backs to the wall', we knew how serious the situation was.

If the training at Boldon and now at Etaples was to make us glad to go back to the line, as far as I was concerned it had been successful. Fed up with what I felt to be useless drill, I was eager to be back with my old pals, offensive or not the day could not come too soon but it was not to be. If one could dodge a parade at Etaples one did, as it usually ended in some silly fatigue with no extra reward as far as we could see. On Sunday morning we were called out on parade unexpectedly. With one or two friends we made a beeline for the back of the lines only to be trapped by a Staff Corporal who told us to 'get fell in'. Perhaps after all it was a Church Parade so we all claimed to be Methodists as the C of E were most likely to have a parade.

It was no Church we went to but one of the larger huts to see an Officer of the Royal Engineers who was waiting for us. He was seeking men for transfer to his unit, a branch of the RE's known as the Field Survey Corps. I was not interested and paid little attention to his discourse. Then he approached each man individually with questions as to length of service in France, education and subjects taken during school days. I found myself being told to stay behind when the rest were dismissed. Here was an Officer who knew his job and how to handle men in a sensible manner putting one perfectly at ease as he progressed.

Learning of my schooling and ability in Geometry and my apprenticeship in printing he told me that of all the men here I was the one he particularly wanted. The Corps had a printing section engaged in map production but mainly he wanted men for observation work, spotting enemy guns and it seemed that Geometry had something to do with it.

After hearing more of the work and its prospects I told him I did not feel inclined to transfer, preferring to return to my own unit, where I had so many friends. This rather surprised him and he asked me more about my experiences with them so far.

Saying he thought I was very foolish to reject his offer which meant first a month on a training course at Merlimont, a coastal resort, and then on to a job which was vital to the war effort. Although this was in the battle zone, it had many advantages in better conditions than the infantry had. Oh, I thought, he knows the disadvantages we live under in the PBI!

Would I try it? He suggested that I should and on the condition that if I was not happy about it, I could transfer back again. It was a most unusual offer so with many misgivings and not a little persuasion I finally agreed. So fortune favoured me...or did it? I was to find out.

Very few men can claim to have served in an infantry battalion all through the war as an actual combatant. Sickness, wounds, leave, training courses or transfers may mean his survival. The chances of him to be in every action for the battalion that I belonged to were practically nil. My wound at Passchendaele had helped me to survive the winter campaign, which had been very severe and I could recall many smaller incidents where only sheer luck had saved my life. So many of my good old friends had died, which they might not have done, had they taken some other course. Was it just luck? Why should I still be here when they were gone, I often asked myself. It was in such a frame of mind that I joined the school at Merlimont, amongst strangers again.

The Chateau at Merlimont was our school building, pleasantly situated in its own grounds, with good dormitories so prospects brightened. The course was intensive covering map reading, a little astronomy (which I liked as a subject but always failed), general observation and recognition of enemy guns. It was a very comprehensive course and well put over by good instructors who were surveyors, civil engineers and Royal Engineers.

I now had the rank of Sapper, which earned me an extra shilling a day. The other Sappers came from all units of the service, some being intended as signallers, cooks, drivers etc. I enjoyed the work, finding it very interesting and I had no difficulty in gaining a full proficiency pass in the final examination. I also made new friends and the time passed happily. Discipline was as it should be, strict but sensible, as laid down by our Commandant, a regular Cavalry colonel whom we all respected.

In retrospect the methods of spotting enemy guns and general observation was primitive, wireless being practically nil. Instruments such as the director itself being a service theodolite, together with a stopwatch such as used by the timekeeper at a sports meeting. A field telephone known as a DR, a Field Survey Map of the area covered and a prismatic compass made up all an observation post required. But it worked. We proved that by triangulating on gun flashes or even smoke puffs, enemy guns could be ranged to within five yards under decent conditions and to me this was fascinating.

During the month, our leisure hours in the evenings were happily spent in the Chateau, where we had a canteen of our own and a reception room. Concerts were held every evening, organised by the Sanitary man, an old soldier of Boer War days and known to us all as 'Old Bill'. He was a cockney, probably a navvy in civilian life but with a true cockney humour. Too old for the trenches, he had been given the job of keeping the sanitary arrangements in order, a job he did exceedingly well and cheerfully. He was a great compere and what started as a few songs at the piano by one or two volunteers, turned to sketches and recitals as first one and then another were encouraged to display their talents. The fame of these performances spread to the Officers who joined us after Mess Dinner.

The programmes grew in length until the time came when Bill would announce "The twentieth item on our programme this evening, gentlemen, is a monologue by Private Bloggs of the East Surrey Regiment who will recite 'Gunga Din'."

I well remember Bloggs, usually with a white handkerchief around his throat, performing his monologues, as we tried to suppress our mirth from 'There's a little golden idol to the North of Khatmandu' to the doings of 'Dangerous Dan Magrew', when he regained his seat to loud applause.

Bill's repertoire was inexhaustible and there was never a dull moment in any concert. His rendering of his own parody of 'La Paloma' was a masterpiece of French phrases known to us and fitted perfectly to the music:

"Pourquoi, ete vous fasher avec moi?"

"S'il vous plais, s'il vous plais" He would go on to the end in a baritone voice worthy of any music hall.

The first time I heard it I was to remember it forever and it became a regular request item. His poem, also his own work, was another even though it had a touch of his unsavoury duties included in the text.

"I am going to give you my own contribution of a poem entitled 'On fatigue'," he would say before the opening lines:

"You get up in the morning and what do you see..." and so on. He missed out none of the sanitary man's duties in the protection of the British Army from the scourge of cholera, to the carrying of barbed wire on a wet night on a diet of baked beans, Fray Bentos and tinned stew.

We had two pianists who always began by taking the front and the lid off the piano to give us the full benefit of their prowess at playing duets. Never did a piano suffer as that one did under their crashing rendering of 'Old Comrades' and of course 'Colonel Bogey'. This made up for all the entertainment we had missed in the past.... Happy days!

The war had to be won and after our four weeks we were split up into detachments and despatched to the front. I went by train to

Amiens there to report to Army HQ Section at the nearby village of Boves. I was detailed to join a post already established in the valley of the Noye near the village of Fouencamps. A pleasant valley with the river close by our dugouts which were excavated into a high banking giving us a good shelter from artillery fire to which we were subject. This was the end of the British line south of Amiens; in fact we were overlapping into the French line and had for our neighbours, several batteries of French heavy guns. We saw no British troops for some time apart from our own messengers and the daily transport driver or Officer on duty from HQ at Boves. The observation post was a mile forward on a high ridge giving an excellent view over the enemy lines for some twenty miles.

Briefly, the system of observation posts were at topographical points about three miles apart from north to south, forming the base of any triangle when ruled out on the survey map at HQ at Boves. We were the most southerly of three posts, all connected by land line telephone, maintained by our signalling section and sometimes by ourselves, when a line was broken by shell fire. New maps were printed and constantly checked by the topographers so they were pretty accurate. France had not been surveyed for many years prior to the war and their maps were anything but accurate, almost useless in modern warfare with the use of highly sophisticated guns. All information we collected was sifted and checked to the closest possible degree and sent to Army or Artillery HQ for immediate action or future use.

Whilst all visual intelligence was sought, the spotting of enemy guns was the main objective. This was most effective at night by flash spotting. On one observer seeing a particular flash being repeated from the same spot, he would report it to the other two and HQ. They in turn would observe for the same flash, which must synchronise with a buzzer the first observer uses as each flash is registered, until they seeing the flash and using the buzzer eventually all buzz simultaneously. Meanwhile the plotter at HQ receives not only a buzz but a flash of light from each post on a panel before him, Once he is satisfied that all three are buzzing together accurately, he asks for our bearings. We read these from the illuminated scale on which the director turns. He then plots by protractor and 'Hey Presto!' another German gun is known to us and in due time will receive attention.

By day the flash may not be seen but a puff of smoke can suffice, though it is not as accurate. Failing that, we use sound bearings using a stopwatch and calculating distance by the time interval from flash to the burst of the shell if it can be seen and pinpointed. On occasion by daylight, I could see the actual gunfire, although the other two posts could not, owing to the contour of the ground. Reporting this to HQ I was told that I had got it wrong and to leave off just before the gun fired again. HQ fell silent for a few minutes then the operator came on again:

"Cook" he said "You were right and that gun is firing on Boves. Keep your eye on it, we are going to ground for the time being."

Our team consisted of six men as observers, a cook, signaller and linesman with Corporal in charge. They were good company and we soon became friends. Corporal Coverton was the oldest man; well educated and had been a Civil Engineer and Surveyor. He was nick-named 'Covers' and was respected mainly for his knowledge of the work in hand, his courage in danger, his unflagging energy and devotion to duty. It was obvious that Covers was enjoying his war, He had to visit posts when we were on duty but his real job was at his own little HQ in the valley where he had a telephone. Nothing escaped him as far as observation or intelligence was concerned. If we were shelled, as we often were, especially if the line was cut, he never rested until he knew we were safe, even setting out alone to visit us, repairing the break on his way which was a most dangerous job usually undertaken by the linesman.

'Knocker' West belonged to the Corps of Signals before joining us. He was a cockney hailing from Walthamstow and in civil life was a printer's cutter which was perhaps one of the reasons I liked him apart from his good humour at all times. By no means a scholar, at times he was out of his depth with Covers and some of the others, who had higher education, nevertheless we all liked him. Covers, Knocker and I were inveterate pipe smokers and always willing to share the last few shreds of tobacco or the last match.

Whilst we had all picked up some French and two were fluent but 'Knocker' never got past 'Bonjour Monsieur'. The Frenchmen from the batteries often visited us and we picked up quite a lot of each other's language. One Frenchman, whilst talking to us, took a lighter from his pocket to light his pipe, which had tobacco hanging down like a festoon from the bowl. Petrol lighters had not reached us and matches were scarce so we resorted to a contraption worked by means of a flint and a worsted wick, the latter also in short supply. Seeing the Frenchman's wick reaching from his pipe to his pocket Knocker's eyes lit up and pointing to his own lighter with about half an inch of string, he hesitantly said:

"Monsieur" pause "Avez vous ..er..Avez vous any wick."

Our French friend was momentarily stunned. Wick was not in his vocabulary and he looked to me for help. I interpreted by asking "Qu'est-ce que c'est" pointing to the wick.

"Ah! Le fabrique" he responded and cut about a foot of worsted off, which made Knocker's day. We were careful not to laugh if a Frenchman was involved, in case he took offence but when he had gone Knocker said to me:

"By Jove Cooky, you are good at French. Thanks very much." Our friends had a good laugh at our expense!

The Observation Post was merely a split trench dug near the lip of the hill with a covering of corrugated iron and a layer of sandbags camouflaged. To approach it by day one had almost to crawl as it was in full view of the enemy should he look our way. Behind us lay a field of corn and immediately behind that a battery of French 75's, their famous field guns. When they fired, the shell skimmed our heads seemingly and brought occasional reply from Jerry so we had it both ways. Hours of duty were from sunset to dawn or dawn to sunset. Two men manned the post, one with a telescope and headphones and the other with signal pad and telephone. With the weather being fine and nothing unusual in the way of enemy activity, we could pass the time quite pleasantly. This was improved when the French engineers came and made us a proper dugout, sinking a shaft some twelve feet deep and excavating a space below for a table, camouflaged with netting and scrim which the French do so well. The observer sat on a plank across the hole with his legs dangling and his instruments before him. They also brought us a very good telescope theodolite, much better than we had with a wide field of view and good magnification, whereas ours had very little at all. On a clear day everything to the skyline twenty miles away was open to view and we had much to report at times. In spite of their attempt at concealment, it was sometimes possible to see the German gunners at work, from our position. Perhaps the strangest thing I ever reported was a band leading a column of Germans along a road, the drummer being very distinct. Howard, my partner confirmed this as I called him to look before I actually phoned in. In spite of this HQ took it as a joke even asking me what tune they were playing. They also would not accept my sighting of a battery and its crew as the other posts could not locate it.

Later I was to confirm my report as we advanced and came upon the battery well and truly crushed just where I said it was.

Life back at the billet was comfortable and relaxing with the trees in the valley still standing and the river very good for bathing. I even learned to swim, something I had never been able to do before. Food was good, our cook being another cockney from East London. Franklin was an excellent provider. He had been a barman before his army days at East Barnet. Like myself, he was a wartime soldier and had seen as much action as I had. He was a good companion and a tower of strength in an emergency. We had to dash for cover occasionally when very high calibre shells fell close by, seeking the batteries which were our immediate neighbours. We considered ourselves fortunate in being protected by the high bank, as the greatest danger was to be caught in the open or from a howitzer which had an acute descent. Our cookhouse was also our dining room built from the bank with a simple roof, furnished with a table and chairs from the abandoned village nearby. Many happy hours were spent playing cards until the day came when a very large shell interrupted our game exploding 50 yards away. We thought from the sound of its flight that the next one might drop short. We heard it coming and scrambled hell for leather along the valley to a French dugout, which was unoccupied. The shell fell right on the cookhouse leaving nothing but a large hole, splintered wood and cooking utensils. We had a lucky escape.

However there is always something to laugh about and this was no exception. One of the visiting French soldiers was Joseph, an artilleryman. He liked to spend time with us improving his English and enjoyed sharing a meal with us as our food was a big improvement on French army fare. We were still sitting in our new dugout until it was safe to return to our own, when we heard:

"Ah, you are here, yes, no and your cookhouse it is broken, yes, no?" Joseph had come to see if we were alright as he had seen the shelling from the gun position. He was quite hurt when we all burst out laughing and went away without another word.

Davey, one of our linguists said we had hurt his feelings by our mirth as the poor fellow didn't understand our sense of humour. He went along to the battery and brought Joseph back. We explained that we had laughed because our cookhouse was not broken but "blown to smithereens". This took some explaining but he was eventually mollified although French humour does not match ours.

As time went on the valley became hotter particularly at night when we got a few showers of gas shells and became more cautious in our movements and swimming trips. During the long days of summer Howard and I were taking a short cut through a cornfield in daylight when we were spotted by a German plane and it chased us with machine gun fire, which gave speed to our legs as we ran for cover.

These things we forgot in the lighter moments when we were given freedom from our duties. Davy and I were even allowed to go to the nearest occupied village to do some shopping at a small estaminet which sold a few bottles of wine but little else.

Davy was a Cornishman and a scholar. He and Rickards, an Armenian, were both linguists. French, German and Dutch came easily to them and they vied with each other as to their prowess in languages. They wanted to learn Russian and sent off to England for primers and once they arrived each took himself off to some quiet corner to study. After a day or two they would meet and we would be regaled with a conversation which was Greek to us but good fun, as Rickards was a peculiar character albeit a scholar from University.

On our shopping trips I walked well in front of Davy for a while, as he seemed to be lagging behind, until a Zouave Colonial soldier challenged me at the point of his bayonet. My cry of "Anglais soldat" availed something but he was very suspicious as no "soldats Anglais" lived hereabouts. He called to a cottage close by and out came a squad of Zouaves who surrounded me. Davy caught up and seeing my predicament entered into a conversation with them in a language I didn't know. Their expressions changed and with smiles all round the danger passed and we were invited for coffee and given as much free wine as we could carry.

I asked Davy how he knew their language and he told me it was Arabic, which he had learned whilst surveying in North Africa in peacetime. He was a man apart and to some of us almost a foreigner himself, but a good pal for Rickards.

Our Officers seldom visited us being in touch by phone, payday being the exception. We only had one payday in the valley which stands out in my memory for the relaxed discipline very different from that which I had been used to. Men who had been on duty all night were usually allowed to stay in bed until later in the day. On this occasion everyone seemed to have been out all night, when Captain Burns arrived on horseback with his groom in attendance. Covers came in to tell us it is payday and the Captain is waiting for us to parade for pay.

"Go and tell him we have been on duty all night and see if he will leave the money and we'll send the pay sheets by despatch runner later. You can handle the money for us alright."

Covers was shaken by the suggestion but seeing we made no attempt to get up he went out and we heard him explaining our suggestion.

"This is very unusual Corporal. Surely they want their pay and it won't take long to do will it?"

Our Corporal made further excuses in his cultured voice and then the reply:

"Well I suppose it is not in regulations but I can pay them where they are and they can each sign the sheet."

With that the Captain entered our dugouts where we were lying in bunk beds and gave us our pay and we sat up and signed with thanks for his consideration of very tired soldiers. We could not have done a very smart parade anyhow under Coverton. He had no idea of drill, nor could he ever present an appearance of an officiating NCO. His tunic hung on him like a sack, trousers well worn and puttees that never did anything but encircle his calves. I think he was glad he had not to do a full parade himself but in spite of his appearance Corporal Coverton was the most valuable man at his job here and we owed him an awful lot.

One more story of Covers may help you to picture the man. It was a very hot day in July, the card school was going nicely, Covers having gone off on some expedition against the enemy as was his wont. He suddenly appeared hot and dusty and picked up a petrol tin standing amongst others, which were used, for carrying water. Lifting it to his mouth he took a good long drink, put it down and cried.

"Good gracious, I've drunk paraffin" and almost changed colour.

Someone had put the paraffin can amongst the water carriers; a daft thing to do at any time and he being badly in need of a drink, would naturally expect it to be water. We all felt sorry for the poor chap as he must have swallowed the best part of a pint and no one could foresee the consequences. All we could advise him to do was to be very careful when he lit his pipe and with this he left us and went to lie down and wait. Fortunately he got over it without undue trouble and being Coverton no one was even admonished for what had occurred.

The hot weather brought its troubles to me when I was on duty with Knocker at the OP. We had taken for rations a tin of MacConacky to share for lunch. On piercing the tin it gave signs of being a bit 'off' but thinking it was very slight, we decided to take a chance. After all these tins were known to have a flavour of their own being a mixture of meat, potatoes, rice and what else we did not know. It was never a favourite with anyone as I remember but we soon felt its effects as we both had violent diarrhoea. Our only lavatory was the cornfield behind us and as the enemy was active too it was no place to linger. Our visits soon used up a copy of the 'News of the World', plus the greater part of our signal book. It was two very uncomfortable men who were relieved that night and next day Knocker came to me saying:

"If some German plane takes a photograph of the post, they will think it is some bleedin' fish and chip shop there."

The weeks passed by, action on our immediate front being confined mainly to artillery fire in the region of Villers-Brettonneux. There was growing activity in the air as both sides sought to gain supremacy but we knew that this could not last. Either we must make a push or wait until the Germans recovered from the reverses and casualties they had suffered in the March offensive, yet still holding much of the ground they had gained. Being more or less isolated in our valley through which very little traffic passed, with only the French artillery as near neighbours, we saw nothing of the vast preparations being made behind the lines. An occasional visitor, the despatch rider or the Topographical Surveyor, would tell us a little but it was always more or less hearsay and second-hand to them. Nor did our French friends know any more so we carried on as usual well into July.

Rumours still abounded but with some signs of big things pending we speculated who might be on OP duty when the attack began but if HQ staff knew any more they were not telling us. The Germans too were guessing.

On the night of 7/8 August 1918 Howard and I went on duty at 7pm and adjusting our headphones, had not long to wait before we heard HQ at Boves enquiring of Covers as to who was on duty tonight. Having given our names the Captain said "Good" and that was all but it had an ominous meaning. We all knew that this must be the big push at last so Howard and I speculated on our part. It was a quiet night for the artillery on both sides with an occasional flash here and there but there was a strange rumbling sound as of heavy transport in the valley below us that we had never heard before.

As dawn broke, the silence was broken as every gun for miles around opened up as one. Synchronisation was perfect, it was like switching on an electric light bulb in a dark room. Immediately the whole panorama in front of us was revealed in a red light as thousands of guns flashed and shells exploded. Here on our hilltop it was as calm as a Sunday morning except for the noise. Not a shell or a bullet disturbed us whilst below men in companies and battalions were being blown to bits. The telephone rang and the CO at Boves spoke:

"No 3 Post, I don't want you to send any reports now this has started. Just sit tight as you are and await further orders." With this Howard and I stepped out of the Post and stood on the crest watching the spectacle before us.

The remarkable thing to us was that all our guns were in front of us. The 75's had, with every other portable piece, moved up in the darkness and taken position almost in the old front line, only a long distance Naval gun seemed to be working in our rear, its shells passing over on its way to a target many miles away. The Germans must have been stunned with the shock of losing practically all their field guns in the first blast. No doubt this was in some measure due to our spotting and registering their positions accurately and to the excellent work of our mapmakers and their painstaking surveys, without which nothing like this could have been achieved. We are apt to forget these silent services and too little praise is given to them for their work.

We watched the infantry advance and in the distance, through telescopes, saw the enemy guns being hastily harnessed to horses and taking flight leaving their ammunition behind. The majority had been put out of action with the gunners lying dead around them, as we were to see later.

Word came to us to go back to billet in the valley, so we packed everything up and leisurely carried the lot and left the dugout, which had served us so well, and an Observation Post the enemy had never discovered. We had reason to believe he had suspicions as there had been one occasion when an enemy plane came very low over us. As he circled so low I could see the pilot looking down. The 75s behind us let fly and the plane rocked like a stricken bird. Pieces flew off his wings but he made away, not before I saw an object like a piece of cardboard fluttering down. Running to pick it up I beat a Frenchman from the battery, also on the same errand. He asked me to hand it over but I refused saying it would go to my CO and eventually to HQ. It was indeed an airman's map and examining it carefully, at the spot on which we stood there was a red query mark. Imagine the surprise at Boves when Cook reported he had just captured an airman's map and on being asked where the airman was being told he had gone home. The Captain came on the line to ask me what tomfoolery this was but hearing the full story congratulated me and told me on no account to part with it to the French. Captain Burns himself came to collect the trophy.

German Observation balloons had always been in numbers on this front. Recently they had increased in spite of the good work of our airmen in destroying them but this morning they hadn't a chance. Once off the ground they pounced and a column of smoke and flame put paid to them.

Whilst we waited in the valley for further orders ready to move, the wounded began to come along, mostly walking but with occasionally a horse drawn ambulance. The majority were French colonial troops with here and there a Frenchman in field blue in contrast to their khaki. Franklin was soon busy making dixies of tea, well sugared and it was welcome to many of them as they rested beside us, accepting what food we could spare. It seemed to us that the Zouaves or whatever they were, were getting a raw deal struggling along on foot, many badly wounded, whilst the blue clad men rode the ambulances some smiling as sitting cases only. Our chef told the Frenchmen to clear off whilst he liberally served his new found coloured friends.

The Maltese cart arrived from Boves and we packed up and left in the afternoon, to join up with the other posts and HQ staff and marched forward to the East. Now we saw at close quarters, the devastation the bombardment had made. Guns and wagons lay smashed to pieces, houses and shelters devastated and dead bodies everywhere one looked. It was interesting to see at close quarters things we had only observed at a distance, as for instance the battery I watched alone. There it was, just as I had said, sunk into the side of a road with a camouflage curtain screening it from the other posts. It was still there but useless, its crew lay dead around it, leading me to wonder if after all someone had believed me and taken my map reference as correct. As we moved on, the roads became busy with supplies going forward and the wounded coming back were now British, as we seemed to have left the French. Actually we were the only post overlapping their lines. Shelling started from German guns fighting a rear-guard action aimed at the roads but it was obvious to all that the collapse of the German Army had begun in earnest.

The sheer weight of our artillery, with superiority in the air, could not fail this time.

At the end of the day having marched eight or ten miles, HQ was established in a house evacuated but still in good condition. Until this day civilians had occupied these houses. Now they had fled and it was some considerable time before we caught up with any of them still in residence.

The three posts took off in different directions to establish observation again. This was the rule, to follow the army as closely as reasonable and establish ourselves at any vantage point- house, church steeple and on one occasion a factory chimney. As we moved, we trailed telephone wire, uncoiling as we walked along. Where he could the linesman would protect it, probably erecting a pole but usually it was left to chance that it would not fall foul of transport or feet. Breakages were frequent but we coped somehow and it was always our first concern to repair a broken line where we could.

The worst night I had was in a village called Montbrehain where we had made our OP in the steeple of the church. It was a pointed spire and we removed slates very near the top for the telescope and fixed a plank to sit on and a shelf for the instruments. A ladder was the only means of ascent and the observer sat with his legs dangling into space. This would have been alright if we had had a good field of view but the village was right on the main road and transport flowed through day and night. It was just the place for Jerry to calibrate his guns on and he never flagged. It was long distance stuff of a very high velocity, a scream, an explosion then devastation with no interval between. However we took our chance and carried on but when darkness fell there was a new terror. German Gotha bomber planes came droning over and dropped their loads on roads and villages, Montbrehain seeming to be a particular target. Nor did this deter their gunners who pounded us heavily. Our communications were soon gone and when a large piece of shrapnel hit the instrument board I thought it was time to seek a better hole. Down the ladder I shot, where Howard was sitting beneath the stone steps leading to the organ still wearing headphones and there we sat until daybreak. There was a constant sound of traffic making a dash for it through the village, with bombs and shells gradually destroying everything including the church itself.

Daylight brought little relief and at last the Gothas gave up. Someone called inside the church and we looked out to see one of our linesmen who had been out all night trying to make connection with us. His lines were broken beyond repair.

On leaving our hideout we found the village destroyed by the night's attacks. Dead horses and men littered the road but still the endless stream of supplies was going through and all were in hot pursuit of the enemy. We were well used to shellfire of all kinds but were meeting a new type of shell, which the enemy was using with an instantaneous fuse. This burst immediately on impact leaving practically no hole. The shrapnel spreading for a considerable distance. If one was caught in the open there was little chance of escaping serious injury or death. An artillery man told me we were using such a fuse which was so delicate that to fire from behind trees was very dangerous as even a twig could spark it off.

This was open warfare and there was no let up as we advanced; seldom using the same posts two nights running. Aerial activity was constant too, with our planes outnumbering the enemy and dogfights above us became so commonplace that we ceased to watch. A trail of black smoke denoted another victim shot down, not always a German and our lone fighters were not alone for long. There was usually another plane to help if he looked to be in any difficulty. It looked as though we had planes and shells to spare.

Although we were constantly on the move we managed to live fairly well. Franklin kept us well fed and we always managed to find some place to sleep, even if only for short spells. The only break I had was in the influenza epidemic which was world wide, coming from the East and claiming thousands of lives as it swept country after country like the plague.

One night Willis and I were at the gable end of a deserted factory which was a good observation point. We were congratulating ourselves on escaping the 'flu which was playing havoc amongst various units with streams of men reporting sick and being sent to hospital. However we must have picked up the virus, perhaps in this very factory which we now occupied but by dawn we both felt very ill and were glad to see the doctor, along with many others. I was running a very high temperature and we were both ordered to hospital at once.

Being in the British lines now we had the comfort of a British hospital train and its excellent staff. Next day we reached Rouen and were placed on stretchers in a marquee because all the wards and beds were full, mostly with cases of influenza who were waiting to be returned to England. That was not to be my luck, by morning I was smoking my pipe.

"How can you smoke? Willis said "I feel as if I'll never smoke again." The duty Medical Officer came on his rounds checking temperatures and deciding who to send to England there and then. Glancing at my thermometer he pronounced me A.1 to return to my unit. I must have been fitter than I thought. I had noticed that gas did not affect me as it did others. To me it was just a peculiar smell.

Hospital transport does not take men back to the line. This time I made the journey back in the van intended for '40 men 8 horses' along with men from the Chinese Labour Corps, or 'Chinks' as we knew them! We had seen thousands of them working on the roads and railways but now we were to see them much closer. It was obvious they were as interested in us as we were in them. Perhaps they thought they were honoured to be travelling with two British soldiers. Their English was non-existent, the limit of their vocabulary being 'GoodeeLa' and 'No goodee la' anything else being sign language. One man sat very close to us and was very interested in our badges. I wore two gold stripes on my cuff having been twice wounded and two blue chevrons for length of service in France. His chief interest was in the distinguishing badge we wore on the top of each sleeve, an blue oval, with the letters FSC embroidered in red. He fingered this, muttering to himself and then examined his own badge, which was similar with the letters CLC. Finally with a look of real delight he exclaimed to his friends, "Goodee-la, Goodee-la."

We were flattered as they accepted us into their corps, if only temporarily. They seemed to eat continuously, the floor of the van was littered with bully beef tins and a constant stream was thrown through the open doors. A spoon appeared to be the only utensil needed as they shovelled tin after tin into their mouths. The journey took twenty-four hours and when we left them, to a happy and vociferous farewell, they were still eating bully beef. They must have raided a wagonload of the stuff. When we reported to the Railway Transport Officer he apologised for our having to travel with them. Evidently he would have found us better company but actually we didn't mind. It was an experience and in their way they were a happy crowd, never quarrelling between themselves. Where they came from I don't know but they did a very useful job as labourers and many must have given their lives for our cause.

To see one of their units on the move was quite a sight and they often passed near our camp. First would come a British Officer with a Chinese NCO just walking along. At irregular intervals his troops followed in ones, twos or threes, ambling along each with a long pole across one shoulder, with his wardrobe and possessions dangling from each end. They looked more like French onion vendors than soldiers. Occasionally one would have a canary in a cage travelling on the end of the pole. Whilst they had full khaki issued they seemed to prefer to wear army woollen 'Long Johns' instead of trousers. With their perpetual grins, they would stop anywhere to 'look-ee' at anything of interest; a motor car, a gun, or our cookhouse. There was evidently plenty of time to get to wherever they were going. Once they came to see some of our fellows in a stream and they could not resist joining in. Down went their poles and just as they were they jumped in, then left to wander on with their wet garments drying on their bodies.

If the leading Officer passed our billet at breakfast his men were still passing at teatime. The railhead used them as shunters and to see one use a shunter's pole equalled a circus act. He would unlink a moving wagon and with the pole sticking out from the buffer he would jump up and lie across it as the wagon hurtled on its way. How many lost their lives in such a mad enterprise one can only guess, but they all did it.

By the middle of September we had reached the famous Hindenburg Line near St Quentin. Our positions were now more often on open ground, selecting a rise or mere hummock in the ground to give us any advantage of view. Spotting had to be done quickly as the German guns were firing and retreating quickly from place to place, so we had to give our artillery information immediately to be of any value. Never before had an army been so defeated as the Germans in 1918. It became a rout but they fought a good rearguard action which was however futile against our numbers and weight of supplies.

If anyone evoked my real sympathy it was the Tank Corps with their lumbering tanks doing about 2 miles an hour. From a very good OP near St Quentin, I watched them going forward with the infantry following, being able to see myself over the rising ground as they went blindly on. If only we had had wireless or some communications with them we could have warned them of what was behind the rise. The German gunners just waited for their appearance and at point blank range, let fly one or two shells and then retreated to repeat it all again. One or two might escape being hit for a time but the destruction of our tanks seemed inevitable and to be hit with high velocity shells at such close range was sheer murder. Two of us watched this, reporting continuously to HQ but there was nothing we could do but watch and hope that at least some might survive but I had grave doubts.

Finally the troops were over the canal and reached the Hindenburg Line itself. The papers at home reported that 'Our army, with the help of tanks, took possession of the Hindenburg Line after fierce fighting' but that did not describe the battle. Where we were, very young lads from Lancashire crossed the canal under fire, without the aid of a bridge. The banks of the canal were cut very deeply and some of the lads who could not swim, improvised water wings from empty petrol cans to cross safely.

Sir Douglas Haig's despatches said 'The 46th North Midland Division (Territorial) who crossed the St Quentin canal at Bellinglise, burst through the German defences and captured 4,000 prisoners and 70 guns at a cost of 800 casualties to themselves.'

I was most interested to meet these lads and hear their story. They were all very young, reminding me of those new drafts we had at Arras and Guillemont, but now they had matured, hardened on the anvil of war and were 'cock-a-hoop' at their success. Why has not someone told this story in detail? It must have been one of the finest achievements of the whole war and by an army of boys.

We spent a few days here before receiving orders to move on, enabling us to see more of these lads and enjoy their company. The Hindenburg Line had been made almost impregnable, with deep tunnels down to two galleries, timbered throughout, with electric light, running water and it was absolutely shell proof. I never liked deep dugouts as men were inclined to lose nerve once they emerged after such security. It affected me this way and no doubt the Germans too, as they were trapped in them once our men reached the opening of the sap. This accounted for the vast numbers who trooped out to surrender in companies and battalions complete with Officers. I had seen a whole battalion at Arras caught this way and they marched in formation to captivity.

Moving on, our future billets were usually in houses with cellars where we often slept on the potatoes, which were stored there. Shelling still persisted against us. One particular house was well furnished with the most comfortable bedroom complete with bed and eiderdown. It was very inviting but we debated as to its safety for a good night's sleep. Only one man volunteered, Parkinson, a printer friend took the chance against our advice. His argument was that if the house took a direct hit we in the cellar would fare no better than he would and he would have the advantage of arriving in heaven complete with feathers for his wings!

Although the village was well and truly strafed he told us that he had slept very soundly.

It was during that period that we had our first sight of the Americans. Pratt and I had chosen a German pillbox as our OP, fixing our telescope on the flat concrete roof and with telephone and apparatus in the box itself, felt quite pleased. Whilst the concrete structure was entirely above ground it had been well built and only a direct hit was feared.

Towards evening an American Officer came with a British Officer, seeking billets for American troops due any time. The American calmly told us that we will have to vacate our new home so that his men could use it. I was not having this at any price and told him I was not allowing him or anyone else to move us from a position we had already fixed on the map and reported to my HQ. The British Officer told me that I was speaking to an American Officer and that he could order me out.

I invited them in and picking up the phone asked to speak to our Captain informing him what had transpired so far.

"You did right Cook" he said, "Don't be bullied out. Put him on the phone and let me speak to him."

I could hear the conversation on the other earpiece. He got a real 'flea in his ear' and he didn't like it. Two very crestfallen Officers were walking away with no apology to me. However I called them back and offered to take a few men if it was really necessary, providing that they did nothing to interfere with our duties. They were glad to accept and when they arrived they quickly came inside to avoid all the flying shrapnel which spattered this particular spot.

The strafe was very heavy that night, making it impossible for us to do any flash spotting at all especially from the exposed top of the emplacement. This was reported before our line was finally cut and we could not even send or receive messages. Shellbursts of really heavy stuff dropped within feet and all I feared was a direct hit. This shelter good as it was could not take that.

The Yanks from South Carolina had no idea what war was yet and we found ourselves answering a lot of questions.

"Say, Tommy, what was that?" one asked, as a shell dropped very close and rocked the pillbox.

"A five point nine shell" I told him.

"Say Tommy if that five nine had dropped on top of this place what would have happened?"

"You wouldn't know and neither would I."

"Say Tommy, would it bounce off this pillbox?" another asked.

"Say Tommy, can you tell me where the latrine is?"

"It's under the stars brother and I wouldn't advise you to go until things quieten down."

"Don't you limeys have toilets supplied?" And so it went on all night, between the munching of corn on the cob and chewing gum.

Sir Douglas Haig said in a despatch at the time: 'The American Army is not yet organised. It is ill equipped, half-trained with insufficient supply services and badly lacks experienced Officers and NCOs. However they had a moral effect on the hard-pressed Germans and our people at home, but the war was really won by such as the little lads from Lancashire and others who learned the trade of soldiering from their elders and the hard school of experience.'

My last observation post was in the village of Preux on the edge of the Forest of Mormal. It was now November and we spent the night on duty near the village where fighting continued all night. At dawn, we were told by phone to enter the village and establish a better position in the steeple of the church, which was still standing, the village having been mopped up and was now clear.

We packed up with no delay but approaching the outskirts we could hear rifle fire and exploding grenades. Some dead bodies lay by the road-side and I remarked that they had not been dead very long. As I looked back one of them was sitting up so I returned and saw that he was badly wounded. He had no arms near him to shoot us in the back and I had to leave him. In the village the infantry were still engaged with one or two snipers and were bombing cellars until Germans came out and surrendered. To me it was Bazentin all over again as we skipped across the road and into the church.

There we met an Engineering Officer who told us he had cleared the building of booby traps and strongly advised us to forget the steeple, as there was a gun still in action in the churchyard. We had our orders so we climbed up to the top and looking down saw an 88mm field gun firing the hated whizz-bangs we knew so well. We looked on him from a very different angle and had we had but a few Mills grenades we could have just dropped them on the lot as they worked but we only had our rifles, which were useless.

Discretion bade us go down. The fight ended and we had no further need to ascend. Actually it was the end of hostilities for me but I didn't know it yet. We were told to stand fast as the Germans had retired into the forest followed by a party of cavalry at a leisurely pace and as far as I remember, not another shot was fired.

Two days later at breakfast, we heard and saw a party of French cavalrymen ride past cheering and crying:

"La guerre fini, la guerre fini ce matin, onze heures. Les Allemandes partie, napoo, kaput, fini!"

We stood, hardly able to believe our ears.

Parfitt, our despatch rider, came riding in.

"It's true lads" he said, "It's all over, there is an armistice at 11o'clock. It's posted up for you to read at HQ in the village." Like one man we trooped down to read for ourselves. Yes, it was official, at the eleventh hour on the eleventh day of the eleventh month it had arrived at last.

> The strife is o'er, the battle done;
> The victory of life is won,
> The song of triumph has begun,
> Hallelujah!

All rejoiced but I remember no cheering as we read and re-read to be quite sure it was all true. We had been through so much and memories of lost friends dulled our rejoicing. Trafalgar Square was a long way off. We would read of their cheering and jubilation later.

Only one man looked disappointed. Corporal Coverton had finished the job he loved, chasing the Hun. He had been a tower of strength to us many a time but if ever a man enjoyed his work it was Covers. We actually had to cheer him up until he became reconciled to the idleness, which was now ours. The perfect gentleman and the perfect warrior!

Our subsequent movements are of little significance; to me it was a well-earned holiday. Knocker, West, Pratt, Howard and others kept together as we travelled into Belgium to Charleroi and finally Namur, a beautiful city where we lived in comfort in civilian billets until final demobilisation. It was February before I arrived home to start life again.

At Clipstone camp I exchanged my khaki for a suit of civvies, fit only for gardening and as I left I thought of my old friends right back to St Eloi days, who were the salt of the earth and I said to myself.

"COOKY – YOU WILL SOLDIER NEE MAIR."

GLOSSARY

ASC	Army Service Corps
CB	Confined to Barracks
CSM	Company Sergeant Major
RAOC	Royal Army Ordnance Corps
RAMC	Royal Army Medical Corps
MO	Medical Officer
HQ	Headquarters
Sgt	Sergeant / Serjeant
SB	Stretcher Bearer
YMCA	Young Men's Christian Association
PBI	Poor Bloody Infantry
NCO	Non-commissioned Officer
VC	Victoria Cross
DCM	Distinguished Conduct Medal
DSO	Distinguished Service Order
Pte	Private

RP	Regimental Police
Limber	A two-wheeled vehicle, originally pulled by four or six horses, behind which is towed a field gun or caisson.
Verey/Very light	Aerial flares used on both sides to watch enemy activity at night or to illuminate no man's land.
Stokes gun	Stokes mortar / trench mortar invented by British engineer Wilfrid Stokes in 1915.
Whizz-bang	A field gun shrapnel shell fired a close range.